DHARMA ART

DHARMA ART

CHÖGYAM TRUNGPA

EDITED BY JUDITH L. LIEF

SHAMBHALA • *BOSTON & LONDON* • 1996

Shambhala Publications
Horticultural Hall
300 Massachusetts Avenue
Boston, Massachusetts 02115

9 8 7 6 5 4 3 2 1

First Edition

Printed in the United States of America

♾ This edition is printed on acid-free paper that meets the American
National Standards Institute Z39.48 Standard.

Distributed in the United States by Random House, Inc.,
and in Canada by Random House of Canada Ltd

Library of Congress Cataloging-in-Publication Data

Trungpa, Chogyam, 1939–
    Dharma art/Chögyam Trungpa; edited by Judith L. Lief. — 1st ed.
        p.   cm. — (Dharma ocean series)
    ISBN 1-57062-136-5 (alk. paper)
        1. Buddhism and the arts.   I. Lief, Judith L.   II. Series:
Trungpa, Chogyam, 1939–   Dharma ocean series.
    BQ4570.A72T78   1996   96-14961
    294.3'375—dc20   CIP

CONTENTS

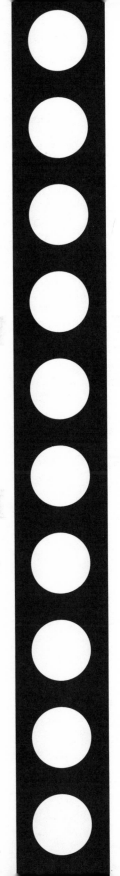

ACKNOWLEDGMENTS

First, I would like to thank the many people who helped in the preparation of this book: Carolyn Gimian and Diana Church of Vajradhatu Archives, Gordon Kidd of Kalapa Recordings (formerly Vajradhatu Recordings), and especially Emily Hilburn Sell of Shambhala Publications. Also, I would like to acknowledge the ongoing work of Vajradhatu Publications, which produced the visual dharma sourcebooks and the many transcripts that formed the raw material for this book, and Ruth Astor, who transcribed and did an initial editing of the Naropa Institute course "Iconography of Buddhist Tantra," taught by Chögyam Trungpa.

For helpful suggestions and advice, I would like to thank Miriam Garrett, Carolyn Gimian, Sarah Sadowsky, David Rome, Ken Green, and Liza Matthews. I would also like to thank my husband, Charles Lief, who came up with the talk title "Art in Everyday Life," in a conversation with the Vidyadhara during the 1973 Vajradhatu Seminary. I would also like to thank the many people who have been working closely with the principles of dharma art over the years, especially the wonderful faculty of the Naropa Institute.

Finally, I would like to thank Mrs. Diana J. Mukpo for her continued encouragement and support of the Dharma Ocean Series.

This book introduces Vidyadhara the Venerable Chögyam Trungpa Rinpoche's teaching on meditation, perception, and artistic expression, which he termed dharma art. *Dharma* means "norm" or "truth." In the context of art, it refers to "the state before you lay your hand on your brush, your clay, your canvas—very basic, peaceful, and cool, free from neurosis." *Art* refers to all the activities of our life, including any artistic disciplines that we practice. It is not an occupation; it is our whole being.

In a meeting in 1982 with the Naropa Institute arts faculty, the Vidyadhara referred to artistic practice as ongoing and all-pervasive. For instance, if you are a musician, you are a musician always, not just while you are playing your instrument. Your awareness of sound and silence is a twenty-four-hour practice. It applies to the way your knife clinks in a restaurant, the way the car door closes, the way somebody sneezes.

In Tibet the Vidyadhara studied a variety of traditional artistic forms, including monastic dance, poetry, calligraphy, and thangka painting. He liked to tell stories of the rigor of his dance training, in which he would need to hold his arm aloft for hours beating a hand drum, until his arm would swell up and he would reach the point of exhaustion. In later years, despite his partial paralysis, he could still demonstrate dance moves from his early training, including dances from the folk tradition as well.

When Trungpa Rinpoche came to England in 1969, he thoroughly immersed himself in the study of Western arts and culture. His interests were wide ranging, including architecture, photography, painting, writing, theater, and music. He also pursued an interest in Japanese arts, including calligraphy and flower arranging, which he studied with Stella Coe of the Sogetsu School. In 1969, while in England, he published *Mudra,* his first book of poetry. Through his new wife, Diana Mukpo, an accomplished equestrian, he developed an appreciation for the art of dressage. Throughout his seventeen years of teaching in North America, the Vidyadhara actively pursued his artistic disciplines and followed his far-ranging interests with immense inquisitiveness and delight.

The Vidyadhara practiced calligraphy on a regular basis and created numerous calligraphies, primarily for his meditation centers and as gifts for students and friends. At the time of taking the refuge vow and again at the time of the bodhisattva vows, students would each receive an original calligraphy of their dharma name. Occasionally he would donate calligraphies to be used in fund-raising auctions. He illustrated points in his dharma art seminars by executing spontaneous calligraphies on transparencies that could be displayed to the audience by means of an overhead projector. In that way, the students could see the process as well as the final result. In his calligraphy, the Vidyadhara worked with Japanese brushes rather than pens, often combining Japanese brush and ink with Tibetan language forms. Such a fusion of forms and methods from different cultures—primarily Tibet, China, Japan, India, England, and North America—characterized his style.

Poetry was a regular and ongoing aspect of the Vidyadhara's daily life. Most often, he would create spoken poetry spontaneously, in informal small group settings. He seldom wrote his poems down; instead, students would transcribe his poetry as he recited it. He often invited his students to participate as well, contributing whole spontaneous poems or lines of group poems. In meetings with the Naropa writing faculty, the Vidyadhara introduced a number of traditional Tibetan writing exercises, based on threefold logic. He encouraged the tradition of spontaneous recitation and the experience of being on the spot without the support of a written text to follow.

When Trungpa Rinpoche came to North America in 1970, he met many artists and poets, and a number of his early students were accomplished artists, such as the poet Allen Ginsberg, the dancer Barbara Dilley, and the musician Jerry Granelli. He also made a close connection with Shunryu Suzuki Roshi, Maezumi Roshi, and a number of other Zen teachers and so continued his interest in the link between Zen and tantra and in Japanese style. He brought with him from Great Britain a great appreciation of English style and design, discipline, etiquette, ceremony, and court forms.

The Vidyadhara also loved to go to the movies and to both observe and create theater. In 1973, the Vidyadhara directed a theater conference in Boulder that attracted many pivotal figures, including Joe Chaikin of the New York Open Theater and Jean-Claude van Itallie. He subsequently formed an ongoing theater workshop called Mudra Theater Group. Working with Mudra Theater, the Vidyadhara developed a sequence of awareness exercises called mudra space awareness practice. He also wrote and directed several plays, including *Prajna, Kingdom of Philosophy, Child of Illusion,* and *Water Festival.*

The Vidyadhara pursued his interest in filmmaking in many ways. In the early seventies, he hosted the Milarepa Film Workshop, to discuss filmmaking and develop a film based on the life of Tibet's poet-saint Milarepa. With a small group of filmmakers, he traveled to Sweden to visit the Museum Ethnographia, where a series of magnificent Milarepa *thangkas* had been stored for years but seldom seen the light of day. The museum staff graciously agreed to pull out the thangkas for viewing and gave permission to the Vidyadhara and camera crew to both film and photograph the entire collection. Unfortunately, although much work was done to develop the Milarepa film, it was not completed due to technical problems with the film. However, the technology now exists to correct these problems, and the film may be completed at some future date.

In the late seventies, the Vidyadhara encouraged the development of a for-profit film company called Centre Productions in Boulder, Colorado. Through Centre Productions, he worked on the direction and part of the actual filming of *Discovering Elegance,* a film based on the process of setting up his environmental installations. In early meetings with the Centre Production staff, the Vidyadhara discussed principles of dharma art as they applied to filmmaking. At the request of his students, he expanded on these informal talks in a series of public seminars on dharma art which form the basis for much of this book. In the eighties, the Vidyadhara worked with Centre Productions on a film about the life of the Karmapa, called *The Lion's Roar.*

In his approach to art, the Vidyadhara stressed collaboration as opposed to solo endeavors. He was well aware of the danger of ownership in art and the problem of feeding ego through art. He discouraged his students from clinging to their identity as artists and encouraged them to think bigger and more inclusively. He also encouraged artists to establish communities. Two artistic communities were formed in the early seventies under his auspices: Padma Jong in Northern California and the Boulder Craft House, which formed the first artists' cooperative in the Boulder area. The Vidyadhara also was involved in the development of a commercial design firm in Boulder, called Centre Design Studio, and served as board chairman. He was an active participant in a variety of design projects under the auspices of Centre Design, most notably the design of a local jewelry store called Kensington's.

Trungpa Rinpoche paid meticulous personal attention to all aspects of the design of his centers, from corporate logos and lapel pins to architecture and furnishings. As his organizations grew and matured, he delegated many things to his senior students, but he rarely delegated design work. He did not view such work as merely decorative, but as having power to direct the energy and set the tone of the whole enterprise.

Having been brought up in a culture where you can take down your tent, roll up your thangkas and rugs, travel to a new location, and quickly set up an elegant and sanctified space out of nothing, Trungpa Rinpoche translated the flavor of nomadic tent-culture into a Western context. He designed a series of calligraphed banners and standards that were displayed in his centers internationally. In designing meditation halls for his Western students, the Vidyadhara was very much influenced by Western Zen, and incorporated both Tibetan and Japanese elements. For instance, he used the round Japanese sitting cushions called *zafus,* but he had them made in red and yellow, rather than black or brown as in Zen. Later, he developed his own unique style of meditation cushion, called a *gomden,* which is placed on top of a traditional small Japanese mat called a *zabuton.*

Trungpa Rinpoche continually exhorted his students to respect the forms of their own culture and not to succumb to fascinations with things Eastern. In preparing for the visit of a leading Tibetan dignitary, His Holiness the Gyalwa Karmapa, in 1974, he encouraged his rather scruffy students to observe proper Western decorum: proper posture and table manners, suits and ties, haircuts, dresses. At the same time, he gave a crash course in Tibetan manners. He wanted his students to be equally at ease with the conventions of tea drinking English style or in the style of the salty butter tea of Tibet.

Trungpa Rinpoche worked with the details of the environment and at the same time with the details of personal dignity and decorum. In this regard, he introduced a series of lapel pin designs, which over time became numerous and elaborated, with each club or organization having its own design. Trungpa Rinpoche did not view these pins simply as identifying symbols, but more like seed syllables, which, though small, contain the essence of the power and magic of the teachings. He did not emphasize form for form's sake, but tried to point out to his students, many of whom had been disillusioned by what they considered the empty and hypocritical religious forms of their childhood, the power of form to teach and to transform. In this sense, he used art all along to convey the essence of things as they are.

In 1974 the Vidyadhara founded The Naropa Institute, North America's only accredited Buddhist-inspired university, and his interplay with Western artists continued. Summer arts festivals blossomed into year-round college in which the arts departments play a central role to this day. Naropa's creative writing department, the Jack Kerouac School of Disembodied Poetics, was formed by Allen Ginsberg and Anne Waldman. Barbara Dilley formed the Naropa Institute dance program. Naropa Theater was begun by Lee Worley. And Naropa's program in world music and jazz was founded by Jerry Granelli and Bill Douglas. The Vidyadhara hoped that one day Naropa would have a full array of fine arts as well as applied arts and crafts, as did Nalanda University in medieval India.

Summers, Naropa hosted an extraordinary gathering of faculty and students and served as a catalytic meeting point for a number of prominent avant-garde artists and performers, including John Cage, Meredith Monk, Jean-Claude van Itallie, Collin Walcott, William Burroughs, Gregory Corso, Robert Frank, Anne Waldman, and Diane DiPrima. The Vidyadhara wanted Naropa to be a spiritual center as well as an artistic center and to host leading contemplatives from the array of world spiritual and psychological traditions. This would provide the ground for what came to be known as contemplative education, in which the various fields of knowledge could be grounded in spiritual depth and creativity.

The Vidyadhara took a great interest in Western music and was especially fond of Mozart and Beethoven. But his musical interests were wide ranging and included the music of China, Japan, India, and Indonesia as well. He wrote a number of songs and often, at the end of programs, joined his students in singing sessions. He worked closely with one of his students, Robert Murchison, in designing and building a large traditional Tibetan drum.

The Vidyadhara's interest in the arts flourished in the late seventies, when he presented a series of flower-arranging exhibits, environmental installations, art exhibits, and seminars on dharma art. He connected the stream of teaching on dharma art with the principles of the Shambhala tradition he was emphasizing at that time. In gathering materials for his installations, he worked with the principle of inherent richness, called *yün* in Tibetan. He trained his students to recognize this quality of richness and power, whether they were selecting the fine art or choosing a tie, and to appreciate the discipline of paying attention to detail.

The Vidyadhara himself paid meticulous attention to every detail of his environmental installations. He would go to the flower market before dawn to pick out the freshest, choicest flowers for his arrangements. He also had the uncanny ability to magnetize people to loan their priceless heirlooms for the installations. Once he came across an eight-foot statue of Yung-Lo which he very much wanted to use in his exhibit. The statue was extremely valuable, and at first the owner was reluctant to part with it. But upon hearing of the Vidyadhara's deep connection with the Yung-Lo lineage of China, he agreed to loan it free of charge.

To help with his artwork, the Vidyadhara founded a group called the Explorers of the Richness of the Phenomenal World, with whom he worked closely to assist in his exhibits and installations, particularly in gathering materials for large flower arrangements. He also founded a school of flower arranging called Kalapa Ikebana. The Vidyadhara also continued to pursue photography and encouraged the development of a photographic society, called Miksang, by his Vajra Regent, Ösel Tendzin.

The dharma art seminars conducted at The Naropa Institute and elsewhere were a rich mix of lectures, discussions, meditation practice, art exhibits and demonstrations, and spontaneous compositions of calligraphy, poetry, and flower arrangement. To give students a simple intuitive exercise, embodying the principles underlying dharma art, the Vidyadhara introduced the practice of object arranging. In this practice, students worked with the placement of simple forms (usually three) in space (usually on a sheet of paper).

In 1980, the Vidyadhara began his association and friendship with Kanjuro Shibata Sensei, the twentieth-generation bowmaker *(onyumishi)* to the emperor of Japan. Through Shibata Sensei, the Vidyadhara introduced *kyudo,* or Japanese archery, to his students and, through Mrs. Kiyoko Shibata, the art of the Japanese tea ceremony as well. With Shibata Sensei he formed the Ryuko Kyudojo group (initially Jvalasara). In the early eighties, he Vidyadhara also formed Kalapa Cha, a society for the study and practice of the way of tea.

Another expression of the Vidyadhara's artistry was the development of a series of festivals for the Shambhala community. In designing the Midsummer's Day Festival in particular, he tried to impart some of the pageantry and ritual splendor of traditional Tibetan folk festivals, with parades, banners, dancing, theater, music, and sporting events.

The Vidyadhara carried his artistry into his home, an idea very much stressed in his dharma art teachings. He took an interest in all the details of his household, including architectural and interior design, landscape design, furniture arrangements, cooking, cleaning, forms of etiquette, dress, and service.

It could be said that in his many teaching activities, Trungpa Rinpoche was always at heart an artist. For many of his students, the essence of what they learned was transmitted through gesture, environment, and artistic creativity. The Vidyadhara's inquisitiveness and love of the great variety of artistic expressions, and his respect for the power of art to awaken and liberate, were unbounded. For that reason, he emphasized the teachings of dharma art for all his students—artists and nonartists alike.

This book is based on a selection of dharma art teachings—courses, seminars, public talks, and discussions—presented in a variety of settings throughout North America. The sources for each chapter are given in the back of the book. May this important stream of teachings awaken our appreciation for the richness of this colorful and challenging world and our compassion to awaken such appreciation in others.

DHARMA ART

Dharma Art — Genuine Art

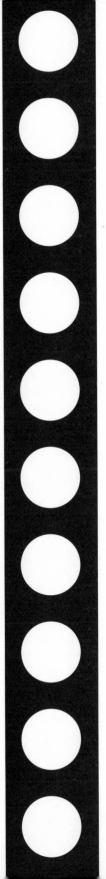

A letter written on the occasion of The Naropa Institute's first summer program, July 1974.

The term *dharma art* does not mean art depicting Buddhist symbols or ideas, such as the Wheel of Life or the story of Gautama Buddha. Rather, dharma art refers to art that springs from a certain state of mind on the part of the artist that could be called the meditative state. It is an attitude of directness and unselfconsciousness in one's creative work.

The basic problem in artistic endeavor is the tendency to split the artist from the audience and then try to send a message from one to the other. When this happens, art becomes exhibitionism. One person may get a tremendous flash of inspiration and rush to "put it down on paper" to impress or excite others, and a more deliberate artist may strategize each step of his work in order to produce certain effects on his viewers. But no matter how well-intentioned or technically accomplished such approaches may be, they inevitably become clumsy and aggressive toward others and toward oneself.

In meditative art, the artist embodies the viewer as well as the creator of the works. Vision is not separate from operation, and there is no fear of being clumsy or failing to achieve his aspiration. He or she simply makes a painting, poem, piece of music, or whatever. In that sense, a complete novice could pick up a brush and, with the right state of mind, produce a masterpiece. It is possible, but that is a very hit-and-miss approach. In art, as in life generally, we need to study our craft, develop our skills, and absorb the knowledge and insight passed down by tradition.

But whether we have the attitude of a student who could still become more proficient in handling his materials, or the attitude of an accomplished master, when we are actually creating a work of art there is a sense of total confidence. Our message is simply one of appreciating the nature of things as they are and expressing it without any struggle of thoughts and fears. We give up aggression, both toward ourselves, that we have to make a special effort to impress people, and toward others, that we can put something over on them.

Genuine art—dharma art—is simply the activity of nonaggression.

Discovering Elegance

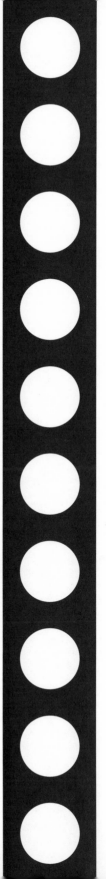

We have to be honest, real, and very earthy; and we need to really appreciate things as they are. They are so beautiful and wonderful already, but in order to appreciate that, it takes time and discipline—so much discipline.

When I was discovered as a *tulku,* which is a Tibetan word meaning "reincarnation of a previous teacher," at the age of seventeen months, I was enthroned as the abbot of the Surmang group of monasteries. At the age of sixteen, I was given the responsibility of governing Surmang district, which had about forty thousand people and covered a large area in Tibet, maybe the size of Vermont. Our province was quite happy and prosperous, and our basic way of maintaining the economy was by exporting timber to the highlands, where there were no trees. The altitude of our place was eighteen thousand feet high. Beyond that altitude there were no trees that could be used for building houses and so forth. There was only shrubbery, small bushes of tamarisk and rhododendrons, and so forth.

The way we led our province and survived our troubles was largely by maintaining farmhouses and the farming life. Everybody owned cattle or, in the English language, what you call yaks. But yak is actually only the masculine, or male cattle; the female is called a *dri.* So there is no such thing as yak's milk. We exported a lot of butter, from nurturing dri and from large numbers of sheep, which were also regarded as tremendous resources.

We exported many different varieties of things, because our province happened to be on the threshold of the highlands and the lowlands. They were not exactly highlands and lowlands from a geographical point of view, since they were all about eighteen thousand feet high; but at the same time, there were mountains and valleys, meadows and plateaus, and high mountain grazing. We produced the best meat, and good cattle (dri and yak). Our particular part of Tibet supposedly produced among the best milk, yogurt, cheese, and butter. The cheese was not produced in the Western style but was just purely part of the milking situation: when there was an early lambing season, cheese was used as part of the diet. We had another type of cheese which was made from powdered tiny sweet potato-type things. We also used underripe grains that were still green and therefore very potent and fresh. It's like the traditional concept of picking young green tea before it becomes fully grown, like some of the green tea from China and Japan. The English type of gunpowder tea is also collected before it is fully matured, so it's fresh and adolescent. Therefore it is very tasty and good for your system. In our province we also had salt lakes. The salt lakes in the Surmang district were not regarded as having the highest-quality salt, but what was called red salt. Groups of people owned particular lakes, maybe a one-fifth-acre salt lake. They worked with the salt lake, scooping out the salt from the water and drying it and so forth. So we also exported salt. That's how we lived in our province.

The monasteries survived on the basis of creating certain funds. Suppose you had a feast or ceremonial time, which might last for ten days—a fund for that particular festivity would be created. When that fund was created, people would be able to make offerings to the monks and to create shrine offerings at the same time. Such a fund might cost, for example, seventy-five sheep and maybe a several-mile-long field of barley and wheat. A person or group of people would manage such an event, and in that way the ceremony could happen. The propaganda that the Chinese Communists put out is not true, from that point of view. What has been said by the Communists is that we flogged our people and squeezed the peasants so that they had to come up with their offerings. That's not particularly true. It's very hard to express truth, I suppose, but as far as I remember myself, that is what we did. At the time there was also the creation of a continuous seminary in our monastery. I looked into the situation, trying to organize the funding part. A fund in that case didn't mean lots of money in the bank or anything like that. Funding meant how many acres of ground that produce grain and how many heads of animals—how many animals to be used for milking and how many sheep for the creation of wool. So in that way, we maintained ourselves.

You may wonder why I'm telling you all these things about how we led our life in Tibet, but I think it has something to do with the situation of

North Americans. In North America, people graduate from college and leave home—or sometimes leave home even before that. There's no sense of home then. They begin to live out of a suitcase and get a job—secretarial, management, depending on their capabilities. People begin to develop an interesting relationship with reality in that way. You don't see how things are produced, what things are made out of, how things have been done. You might see a silk-screened design and like it, so you buy it without knowing anything about the process of silk-screening. Or you might buy a carpet, not knowing the weavers or the carpetry world at all. And when things go wrong, usually we call a specialist.

Dharma art is not so much that you should be artistic, that you should paint a lot of pictures, compose music, or at least play music. And it is not that you should develop some fruition of beauty. That seems to be a problematic situation here, and it was exactly the same in Tibet. If I had not been made governor of my province, I probably also wouldn't have known how things worked. I probably would have taken the same attitude that some of you might have. And I might have said, "Now we're having this festival, so why is this food coming, what's wrong with it?" I probably would have gotten pissed off. But in order to be a governor, and a practical person, I needed to know how successful and luscious and powerful such a ceremony could be, and how it was based on the economy and morale of the people, at the same time.

The question is: How are we going to organize our life so that we can afford to produce beautiful things, not at the expense or the suffering of others? That seems to be the basic point from a practical point of view. Then there is something beyond that, which is the concept of art altogether, or dharma art. It is a question of discovering elegance and dharma art, which may be two slightly different topics. Dharma art comes first; discovering elegance may come later. So dharma art is not showmanship, or having some talent that nobody had before, having an idea that nobody's done before. Instead, the main point of dharma art is discovering elegance. And that is a question of state of mind, according to the Buddhist tradition.

At this point I am talking about the artists, rather than the perceivers of art alone. Traditionally, it is a long and arduous process to produce and manufacture art. For instance, to make paint, somebody has to grind vermilion

5

stone in order to make the color vermilion; somebody has to collect greenery in order to make green; somebody has to grind and work with deposits in a cave in order to make blue; somebody has to collect deposits on the earth in order to make orange. Somebody has to work with the soot coming out of bark or the sap of trees to make ink. Everything is made in that way. Before you get into your fancy work as artists, you have to know the pain and the misery, or maybe deny it, that is involved in producing such a work of art. Take the example of the flowers we use in flower arranging. They do not just bloom in heaven and God just shoves them down to us. They need earth, soil, lots of manure, and the protection of the weather, so that finally we have a beautiful chrysanthemum, beautiful irises.

From the modern American point of view, you can just go to the store and buy things and pick them up. That is not quite a good attitude, let alone elegance. People have to realize how things are made and produced, how they happen to be so beautiful, so lovely. Once something is at its best, its fruition, we tend to neglect that. But we are just starting with spring at this point, we haven't even gone through a summer, let alone autumn. We are far from harvesting. I could say that quite safely. Whether you are the greatest artist who has already made your name and made a good contribution to the world, or at the beginner's level, we have to realize how difficult it is to start the whole thing. We have to work with the ground, path, and fruition levels together. That is not a particularly easy thing to do.

We really have to drop the idea that if we are driving for a long time on the highway and we get tired and the signpost says, "Food, lodging, and blah-blah-blah," we can turn off and check into a motel, go to sleep, eat food, have a good time, and go on the next day. We can't always use our world like that. We have to have some respect for the people who work hard on such situations. We cannot simply say, "Things are fine, convenient; therefore I might as well take advantage of it, as long as I have money." Usually places charge based on how much work they put in and, according to that, how much production they have achieved. But we don't think about that, particularly. As ordinary, regular, naive people, in fact, we might tell our friends, "Such and such a motel is cheaper than such and such a motel." Why is it cheaper? It is cheaper because they worked with prefabrications. At the more expensive hotels, it was more difficult, because they put in more effort and energy to make their place splendid and good. We ignore so much of our practicality.

The medieval world produced fantastic works of art, as you know: music, painting, instruments, and everything. In the medieval world, some of the greatest artists were only known to be great artists after they died, because when they were living, they worked so organically, trying to put things together. When the fruition of their work came along, they were so pleased and satisfied; but at the same time, their energy ran out and they died. So even though you might have talent at an early stage of life, like Mozart, nonetheless art is still a manual process. Everything has to be manual and realistic. Then you discover the elegance and beauty, because you begin to realize how much energy and exertion it takes to manufacture or display the best of the best. That is what it takes for breathtaking music and breathtaking paintings to happen at the fruition level. You don't have that right at the beginning.

If you want to become an artist and you want to have the best of everything, you can't just have it. You have to start by paying attention to reality. You need to learn to eat properly, to cook properly, to clean your house or your room, to work with your clothes. You need to work with your basic reality. Then you go beyond that, and you begin to have something much more substantial. And beyond that, you actually begin to produce a master artistic world altogether. That is the same as in my tradition of Kagyü Buddhism. It is long and arduous; you can't become suddenly good at something. Of course, it is possible that overnight you come up with a good gadget, a good idea; the next day you patent that and begin to manufacture it, and suddenly you become a multimillionaire. That could happen. But we do not regard that as a true way of doing things. We are bypassing a lot of training, discipline, and reality. And often, when people produce a good work of art in that way and make a lot of money suddenly, they end up committing suicide, dead. Just like Marilyn Monroe.

We have to be honest, real, and very earthy, and we need to really appreciate things as they are. They are so beautiful and wonderful already, but in order to appreciate that, it takes time and discipline—so much discipline.

7

Great Eastern Sun

You wait for the good moment—the infamous first thought—but nothing happens. There is a thought of giving up the whole thing, or else trying to crank something up artificially. But neither of those things works. Then you sort of become distracted by something else—and when you come back, there it is!

Involving ourselves with visual dharma seems to be very straightforward: working with oneself, working with others, and working with oneself and others together. Working with oneself brings the realization of one's own elegance. Working with others means trying to develop delight in others. And the two together, elegance and delight, bring a basic sense of richness and goodness, which is known as Great Eastern Sun vision. Obviously, you must know by this point that a work of art brings out the goodness and dignity of a situation. That seems to be the main purpose of art altogether.

Great Eastern Sun terminology is used quite a lot in the Shambhala tradition, which is very ancient, and it is also applicable to the present. The three principles of *Great, East,* and *Sun* have specific meanings. *Great* means having some kind of strength, energy, and power. That is, we are not fearful or regretful in presenting our expressions or our works of art—or, for that matter, in our way of being. That power is absolutely fearless. If we were cowardly, we would have a problem in trying to handle an object, or even thinking of touching it or arranging it, much less in arranging our life or our world. We would be afraid to do any of that. So the absence of that fear is fearlessness, which develops out of delight. We are so delighted that we spontaneously develop that kind of strength and energy. Then we can move freely around our world without trying to change it particularly, but just expressing what needs to be expressed or uncovering what needs to be uncovered by means of our art.

East is the concept of wakefulness. The direction in which we are going, or the direction we are facing, is unmistakable. In this case, the word *East* is not necessarily the geographical direction. Here, it means simply the place you see when you can open your eyes and look fearlessly ahead of you. Since this East is unconditional, it does not depend on south, west, or north. It is just unconditional East as basic wakefulness.

Then we have the third category, or Sun. *Sun* has a sense of all-pervasive brilliance, which does not discriminate in the slightest. It is the goodness that exists in a situation, in oneself, and in one's world, which is expressed without doubt, hesitation, or regret. The Sun represents the idea of no laziness, and the Sun principle also includes the notion of blessings descending upon us and creating sacred world. The Sun also represents clarity, without doubt.

Those three categories are the nature of Great Eastern Sun. We could say that they are trying to bring us out and to uncover the cosmic elegance that exists in our lives and in our art. In contrast, the notion of *setting sun* is that of wanting to go to sleep. Obviously, when the sun sets, you go to sleep. You want to go back to your mother's womb, to regress, appreciating that you can hide behind dark clouds. That is to say, there is no bravery; it is complete cowardice. At the same time, there is struggle: you do not want to step out of this world completely; you are still trying to survive, still trying to prevent death. So the setting-sun world is based on a psychological attitude of fear. There is constant fear, and at the same time it is deliberately suicidal.

We have a lot of examples of setting-sun art. Some of them are based on the principle of entertainment. Since you feel so uncheerful and solemn, you try to create artificial humor, manufactured wit. But that tends to bring a tremendous sense of depression, actually. There might be a comic relief effect for a few seconds, but apart from that there is a constant black cloud, the black air of tormenting depression. As a consequence, if you are rich you try to spend more money to cheer yourself up—but you find that the more you do, the less it helps. There is no respect for life in the setting-sun world. The only respect you can find there is in the brotherhood of human beings who are trying to combat death with the wrong end of the stick. I'm afraid at this point I have to be biased; there's nothing positive I can say about setting sun at all. But that actually helps, in that we can see black and white clearly and properly, so there is no doubt whatsoever.

Obviously, Great Eastern Sun vision does not mean that the good people have to win all the time in plays or films. It is not all that simpleminded. For instance, in the Buddhist tradition, there's a series of stories about the Great Bodhisattva being eaten and recycled, so there is no problem there. That seems to be okay. And the same thing could be said about the Bible, which contains the crucifixion and resurrection, but still continues that vision. So the question of Great Eastern Sun versus setting sun is not so much whether somebody physically wins a victory, but whether psychologically that sense of vision is continued.

The three categories—Great, East, and Sun—are categories of awaking or arising. But I should mention that there is a difference between rising sun and Great Eastern Sun. Rising sun is like a baby; there is potential. The Great Eastern Sun is fully developed, a fully matured sun, whereas the rising sun is an infant sun. So the idea of Great Eastern Sun is to be fully confident and fully developed, full speed ahead. The Buddhist analogy is that buddha nature exists in you, fully developed. You don't have to try to bring buddha nature into you, but you are already fully awake, on the spot.

The Great Eastern Sun principle has three additional categories or attributes. The first is a quality of *peace.* It is permeated with confidence and dignity, that is, nonaggression. The essence of a good work of art is absence of aggression. Sometimes you might find the elegance and dignity so overwhelming that it's threatening, but that has nothing to do with any aggression that exists in that work of art. It is just that you are so cowardly that you get frightened. So you shouldn't regard such an overwhelmingly splendid presentation as aggression.

The second category of the Great Eastern Sun principle is known as *showing the path.* That is, the artist begins to develop some sense of discriminating awareness wisdom in picking and choosing between wholesome and unwholesome situations. We are not just being naive and accepting everything, but some discrimination takes place, which shows the path from the point of view of Great Eastern Sun vision. This showing of the path could be regarded as first thought–best thought. First thought–best thought is not necessarily a chronological event. Quite possibly, the first thought might be the worst thought, chronologically speaking. In this case, first thought refers to that thought which is fresh and free.

In the beginning, there is some kind of gap. After the gap, there is an expression of that gap, which is first thought. It is not particularly vague; rather, it is very definite, extremely definite. And it has discriminating capabilities. For instance, when you have your paper and ink and brush, and you project your Great Eastern Sun vision, at first nothing might come into your mind. You might think that you are running out of inspiration. You wait for the good moment—the infamous first thought—but nothing happens. There is a thought of giving up the whole thing, or else trying to crank something up artificially. But neither of those things works. Then you sort of become distracted by something else—and when you come back, there it is! The whole thing exists there. That little flicker of gap brings you to first thought. Then you have the confidence and dignity to execute your brushstroke, your calligraphy, or your painting. And the same thing could apply to musicians or photographers, or to any artist. So showing the path is a guideline of how to see these situations on the spot, on the first thought–best thought level.

The third category is *victory over the three worlds.* That is somewhat mysterious sounding, but we have to look at the concept of victory. Usually victory seems to mean being able to beat somebody, becoming the best either by sheer pressure, sheer one-upmanship, or sheer knowledge. But from the Great Eastern Sun point of view, the concept of victory is a natural sense of existence that provides no need for challenge, so no enemies exist. Since there is no regret and no laziness, you begin to appreciate the sacredness of the world. Everything is complete and extremely wholesome, so there is no problem. The threefold world is the world of heaven, the world of earth, and the world that joins heaven and earth together, which is your physical body, your speech, and your psychological state of mind. So there is victory over the neuroses of all those realms.

To summarize, the concept of Great Eastern Sun vision is threefold. First is having a sense of goodness in yourself. Second, having some sense of decency in yourself already, you can project that to your audience, your clientele, or the world in general. In that way a tremendous trust is established: goodness, decency, and trust. Third, because all of that has been established, therefore you can create what's known as *enlightened society*—by works of art, by basic sanity, and also by artists beginning to practice sitting meditation. Needless to say, we have to slip that in somewhere.

In the early days of the Western world, Great Eastern Sun artwork was happening constantly. Great Eastern Sun vision appeared not only in a lot of art, but in the lifestyle as well. Then people began to lose the sense of Great Eastern Sun vision, because their dignity was being questioned. Dignity was regarded as purely something to be cultivated, something belonging to the rich and above the heads of the peasants. The noble families had more food to eat than the peasants, and that kind of economic situation led to the Industrial Revolution. Then of course, the notion of democracy came along, saying that all men are equal. This meant that no hierarchy could take place.

Nowadays, on the whole I think that some modern artists are good and sane and have a tremendous sense of Great Eastern Sun vision, but they are extremely rare. There are only a few of them—very few. It is up to you to figure out who. Otherwise, we will be discriminating between good and bad, happy and sad. I think there is a definite trend of Great Eastern Sun vision; it is beginning to pick up. It did pick up in the sixties, though in the early seventies nothing happened at all. Everybody leaned toward setting-sun drama. But now people are beginning to come around and to pick up on it. During the twenties in America, a lot of interesting things began to happen. People didn't know what they were doing, but there were good feelings and real things took place: people actually knew how to conduct their lives and how to produce works of art. Unfortunately, art has now become an economic investment, which is a great obstacle to the artist. It doesn't leave us with very much to work on.

There is also a lot of setting-sun vision in the Japanese tradition. The flower-arranging school I came from is very much a setting-sun school, which I somewhat regret and respect at the same time. You see, the whole point is that we have to develop ourselves first, before we engage in anything else. We can't do very much other than that. We have to develop some understanding of Great Eastern Sun vision first, and then we can go out and study with teachers according to that particular principle. That seems to be the only way.

We can't find any holy land of flower arrangers, or another art form we want to do. We have to find it within ourselves.

In developing Great Eastern Sun vision, I think we have to emphasize the Western tradition as well as the Eastern. In order to inspire American students, I've been working with them in all kinds of ways. I've been telling them how to buy a good tie, a good suit, cuff links, shoes, how to say "Yes, sir" and "Please, may I." I've been training them to behave as good human beings. And it's the same with art. We have to have some understanding of Buddhist Oriental composure, but at the same time we should also have the vision of the Western world, which in itself is quite remarkable. Tremendous things have happened here, but lately everybody has been trying to ignore that and make an amusement piece out of the whole tradition, to cut it down and make it all into a Coca-Cola world. When we do that, we run into problems. But as long as we don't give up our Occidental vision and dignity, I don't think there's any problem. And actually, there is such a thing as the Occidental Great Eastern Sun. That is a linguistic contradiction, like saying that the sun rises in the west, which is a silly thing to say. But the West is west, and therefore the sun also rises in the West, something like that. I myself have been inspired by great artists, painters, and musicians of the West. Therefore I'm here: I'm living in the Western world, and I appreciate my world tremendously.

Basic Goodness

Basic goodness is like a flower arrangement, which has its own contrast and its own togetherness. It is completely together, at the same time both inviting and fearless. There is no premeditation; it just comes along on the spot—basic goodness.

The Great Eastern Sun represents the notion of awake and also the notions of energy, luminosity, and brilliance. Basically, those qualities represent the fundamental state of mind an artist should have. He or she should have that kind of vision and that state of being; otherwise, there are a lot of problems and difficulties. At the beginning, Great Eastern Sun vision is very black and white. When the sun shines, it is white; when the sun doesn't shine, it is black. We have to cut through our ideas of indulging or lounging in the possibility that something might occur simply out of our experience. Obviously, there is room for open-mindedness in Great Eastern Sun vision, since it is basically a state of mind in which wakefulness, enlightenment, and open-mindedness are all involved. But in order to be open-minded, you have to open your eyes much wider, not just glance around, looking at things with half-closed eyes.

This is a very important issue: if you have a completely open mind and open eyes, you can discriminate further, and you can judge the situation accordingly. You are able to say yes to certain things and no to certain things. In fact, quite possibly you could open yourself *further* by presenting yourself and acting on the situation. In that way, as long as you know their dangers and their merits, even questionable subjects could be included. So it is very important for the artist to have that first mind, or artistic mind, which from the Great Eastern Sun point of view is awake rather than half asleep. If you are awake and on the spot, then you can juggle things around. That is basic healthiness and openness.

Having seen the vision of the Great Eastern Sun from a fully awake point of view, we can begin to develop nonaggression. Usually, we are trying to take advantage of our world—to milk our world or to slaughter it. We have precisely the same attitude toward our world that we have toward cows. We take away their baby calves and milk the mothers to make butter and cheese—if they last long enough. And if they don't produce anything, or even if it only looks like they won't produce anything, we slaughter them and eat them up. That is an expression of aggression, which is the setting-sun version of how we view our world—and how we view our art as well. If a work of art is fun and productive, we go on; but if it is not, we give up on it and get into an entirely different subject. So nonaggression seems to be very important.

What makes us blind? Aggression makes us blind, so we can't create visual dharma. What makes us deaf? Aggression creates deafness, therefore, auditory dharma cannot be produced. And because of aggression, dharma touch, dharma smell, or dharma taste also cannot be produced. To use an American idiom, when we are uptight, we are being aggressive. We are so dissatisfied with ourselves, our world, and our work that we begin to feel that everything is worthless. Or at the least, we feel that some things are worthless, while other things might have some worth. We pay more attention and take things so personally that when any negativity occurs in our lives, we get aggressive and uptight. On the whole, we could say quite confidently that aggression makes us blind and deaf, so we cannot produce a work of art, let alone anything else. We cannot run our lives. Aggression makes us dumb mutes, so we become like vegetables. Aggression might produce a so-called extraordinary work of art, but art produced in such a way pollutes the world, rather than producing something refreshing and healthful.

The purpose of dharma art is to try to overcome aggression. According to the Buddhist vajrayana tradition, if your mind is preoccupied with aggression, you cannot function properly. On the other hand, if your mind is preoccupied with passion, there are possibilities. In fact, artistic talent is somewhat related to the level of passion, or heightened interest in the intriguing qualities of things. Inquisitiveness is precisely the opposite of aggression. You experience inquisitiveness when there's a sense of wanting to explore every corner and discover every possibility of the situation. You are so intrigued by what you've experienced, what you've seen, and what you've heard that you begin to forget your aggression. At once, your mind is at ease, seduced into greater passion.

When you are in a passionate state, you begin to like the world, and you begin to be attracted to certain things—which is good. Obviously, such attraction also entails possessiveness and some sense of territoriality, which comes later. But straightforward, pure passion—without ice, without water, without soda—is good. It is drinkable; it is also food; you can live on it. It's quite marvelous that we have passion, that we are not made purely out of aggression. It's some kind of saving grace that we possess, which is fantastic. We should be thankful to the Great Eastern Sun vision. Without passion, nothing can be experienced; nothing can be worked on. With aggression, we have bad feelings about ourselves: either we feel tremendously righteous, that we are the only ones who are right, or we feel pissed off that somebody is destroying us. That is pathetic. It prevents us from seeing the basic goodness.

Basic goodness is like a flower arrangement, which has its own contrast and its own togetherness. It is completely together, at the same time both inviting and fearless. Such a flower arrangement is a product of basic goodness, if I may say so. It hangs together. There is no premeditation; it just comes along on the spot—basic goodness. For instance, I went up to the mountains today to collect some branches and this tree was there, just waiting to be collected. When I saw it I said, "Ah! That will do." We had to work on the tree a little bit in order to transport it, but that is also an expression of basic goodness, of how things hang together. Basic goodness combines the qualities of heaven, earth, and man: basic goodness of heaven, basic goodness of man, and basic goodness of earth are all involved at once. Basic goodness includes generosity and bravery. There is also a notion that all things are round. It is like the mandala principle, in that every single thing is working together with all the other elements, which is why the whole thing hangs together so well. And we begin to feel that way ourselves, that basic goodness exists in us. Therefore, we are not afraid of our world, and we are not depressed about our world. We feel so good.

We feel good about the particular artwork we are doing, and we begin to have further ideas. Some people try to squeeze ideas out as if they were constipated, sitting on a toilet seat, glancing occasionally at the toilet tissue, wishing something would come through. When artists do that, the result is very meek and very technical. They always refer back to technicalities and try to produce something out of that—but they don't really feel good about the whole thing at all. What we are talking about here is the opposite of that. It is not exactly like developing diarrhea, but there is some kind of free flow, in which you have the confidence that you can actually produce ideas. You may not have any ideas at the beginning, but you might get some ideas halfway through. If you don't have any ideas halfway through, or you feel that you have run out of ideas altogether, then you take a short break, almost at the level of giving up. Then the Great Eastern Sun rises in your mind. That is not just an idea—it is something that actually occurs in your state of mind.

Basic goodness is connected with generosity and with a sense of trust in oneself. When that sense of trust comes through, we develop what is known as harmony. If there is no trust, there will be no harmony. It is all very well to say that everything is in harmony and that we should work with that; but that is just paying lip service, saying that something should be done, while nobody actually does it. It reminds me of certain religious conferences I have attended. The first one I experienced was a harmony conference, held in New Delhi while I was living in India. Then there were little harmony conferences that took place in California. They invited rabbis, *bhikshus,* priests, the whole gang. Everybody was talking about harmony, but they didn't find any harmony on the spot. Although they were talking about harmony, there were no results at all. Nothing at all happened, absolutely nothing! People came to the conference and left the conference the same way. But they went back saying, "We took part in a conference on harmony; therefore, our organization is greater now." But how could that be? That's very sad. It verges on setting sun, and it is not even sophisticated but primitive setting sun.

Harmony has to be related to some sense of lusciousness or richness. That is one aspect of harmony. The other aspect is a sense of spaciousness and openness. The lusciousness almost has the qualities of a Jewish mother: it is plentiful, rich, and there is lots of stuff on the table, so to speak. The openness and spaciousness are like a Japanese home, where things are very sparse. There is no big furniture, no Victorian stuffed sofa, just mats. When you sleep, you sleep with a block of wood or even a stone as a pillow. So true harmony is the Jewish home and the Japanese home put together quite conveniently. Technically, we could call that a Shambhala home, or Great Eastern Sun home. And the same kind of harmony could be true of your artwork as well.

When such harmony takes place properly and fully, there is also joy—for the very reason that you are not struggling to create the harmony. In that way, you are also creating enlightened society, which can only exist with that sense of harmony and inquisitiveness and all the other things we've been discussing. It is our duty to create an enlightened society through works of art and through our sanity. And obviously, meditation practice is very important. So in the name of heaven, earth, and man, I bow down.

Meditation

Awareness is very important. We are here, nowhere else. Since we are here, why not be here?

According to Buddhism, art is something produced by a student rather than by an isolated person. You might think that sounds very stuffy; however, it is true. Art is produced by a student with an interest not only in his own creation, but in the basic necessity of expression—that is, what needs to be shown to others. Beyond that, the Buddhist approach to art is anti-garbage. You don't keep churning out scruffy things; they go into the garbage and are burned.

The basic Buddhist approach to art comes from a sense of studentship, which is also a sense of teachership, because even though teachers may be highly developed, they are still always students themselves. One of the reasons that art has never died is that successive teachers have continued to study works of art, rather than just proclaiming themselves as models. Usually what happens to those who proclaim themselves as models is that they lead decadent lives and become cynical and aggressive and indulge themselves unnecessarily.

Basically, when we talk about art, we are talking about a form of some kind that we could work on. So it is like the practice of meditation. But what is that form, and how does meditation go along with it? The obvious answer according to the Buddha is that form doesn't actually exist, and dharma also doesn't exist; therefore, form and dharma could mix together. It's like spreading cheese on bread: you can't distinguish between the cheese and the bread anymore. In order to do that, we need a lot of meditative discipline. Absolutely nobody can become a good craftsman or a good artist without relating with the practice of meditation. By meditation I mean *shamatha-vipashyana* practice, not hunting peacefully in the jungle with your rifle or fishing peacefully, sitting beside the lake with your fishing rod. I'm talking about the sitting practice of meditation. Nobody can create a perfect work of art or understand a perfect work of art without understanding the practice of meditation. So the sitting practice of meditation is the basic ground.

But what do we mean by the sitting practice of meditation? For instance, Beethoven, El Greco, or my most favorite person in music, Mozart—I think they all sat. They actually sat in the sense that their minds became blank before they did what they were doing. Otherwise, they couldn't possibly do it. Just coming out of the market and plopping down at the dining-room table and writing a play—that's impossible. Some kind of mind-less-ness in the Buddhist sense has to take place.

From that basic ground, the sense of being, openness, or *isness* begins to develop. *Isness* might be a better word than *being,* because there *is* something happening. When you sit or you don't sit, when you cook your meal or wash your dishes, there's isness taking place. In the Buddhist tradition, that is called awareness. But we are not referring to the kind of awareness where we say, "I should be aware that I have to take my medicine at five o'clock, since I'm allergic to bugs." It's not that kind of awareness. The awareness referred to here is isness, which is very important and powerful. We have to understand that and work with it. That is absolutely important.

Isness is all-pervasive. Whatever we do, there is something happening. So there is no separation between the medium and you. For instance, if at this moment you are sitting on your buttocks on the floor underneath a tent—that is isness. We are here, we are actually here! That kind of awareness is very important. We are here, nowhere else. Since we *are* here, why not *be* here?

That sense of isness, beingness, or awareness is known as postmeditation practice. In sitting meditation, you don't trip out, but simply sit, identify with your breath, work with your thoughts. You do everything very manually, very definitely, constantly. But in postmeditation practice, you are here. You are definitely here: whether you are combing your hair, pressing your clothes, walking around, taking a bite of a peach, or whatever you are doing in your life. That is all an expression of isness.

In terms of art, if you do art, you just do it. You can see that this part of the clay is wrongly put or this particular color is wrong, so you scrape it out or use another color. You go ahead and do it. There's no problem, and there's no challenge either. Nobody is trying to compete against anything. You are not trying to become the master of the world. You are just trying to be yourself and express yourself in a very, very simple, meditative, and nonaggressive Buddhist way. And as you meditate more and you work on your art more, the boundary between meditation and the practice of art, between openness and action, becomes fuzzy—which is what everybody experienced in the past.

The Buddhist way of approaching art is nonaggressive. Aggressiveness brings competitiveness, money concerns, comparison, frustration, excitement, all kinds of things. If there's no aggression, that brings joy, openness, dance. I don't mean joy in a sense of love-and-light, swimming in a sea of honey—but joy in the sense that things could be touched and appreciated. You could look at things that are beautiful, but there's no point in picking the flower. You can look at things, you can experience things, you can feel things, you can touch things, and that's fantastic. There is a real sense of real richness taking place from that perspective of nonaggression, nonpossessiveness. Some people go window-shopping in big cities, and all the time they are miserable because they can't afford to buy anything. Other people go window-shopping because they like to look at beautiful things. That seems to be the basic distinction.

Aggression is very deep-rooted. Anger is like the heart of the earth: it has brewed for years and years and years, thousands of years. And when it is just about to give a little peep out on the surface of the earth, that is aggression. Don't try to make it go away, and don't try to invite it—that is what's called the path. The path consists of collections of dirt, stones, grasses. It includes everything—passion, aggression, and ignorance. Without those, you have no path. So you shouldn't try to build a highway and have everything smooth under your car. That's the difference between the Buddhist path and the American materialistic path.

One kind of aggression happens because you have stuffed so much stuff into your head and you want to let it out, to make a display of it. Another kind of aggression is competitiveness, being achievement oriented. And yet another kind of aggression is that you are so involved with yourself that you forget the surface of the canvas or the medium that you are working with, so you lose the point. Also, in many cases, art is regarded as a release. That is absolutely the wrong attitude. A work of art should not be regarded as a release! "I have nothing to do, I feel slightly depressed. Why don't I go to the pottery wheel and make some pots? That feels good." It is very sacrilegious to regard a work of art in that way. Art has to be very serious.

Art is unlimited. You can do anything. You can make a stick into a pair of chopsticks. You can do all kinds of things. You do not have to rely on a professional message coming through before you can do it—unless you are working with something complicated, like computers. At the same time, you should be open to an artistic way of viewing that could be very technical and very detailed in terms of symbols and space and so forth. That also comes from the sitting practice of meditation. Usually in art, your medium is based on something very simple and direct. Sometimes there's fear, sometimes obstacles, but you should just go ahead and do it. Buf if you expect your work is going to be great, the result will be that your work is terrible.

In looking at the role of sitting meditation practice in artistic perception, we should try to understand how the practice of meditation changes the way you relate with your world: how it changes your visual system, your hearing system, and your speaking as well. The way you look at somebody depends on your confidence and on how much you want to look at such a person. When you project your voice, it is quite clear to what degree you are willing to expose yourself. So I would like to make it quite clear that what we are talking about is not purely aesthetics. A lot of artists are trying to present something beautiful and nice, flowery, polite. But we are not trying to be overly polite or aesthetic—or, for that matter, overly rude. The idea is that the way we behave and the way we work with our sense perceptions comes from simple and straightforward Buddhism. You could call it buddha nature.

The important point, to begin with, is to have a blank sheet of paper in front of you. That is, you are willing to open, willing to let go. The Buddhist approach to art is not so much learning the tricks of the five buddha families, but having a sense of openness and perspective. Artistic talent and the concept of visual space is already available to you. You don't need to cultivate it, and you don't need to make up something without any context. It happens naturally and very simply. According to the tantric Buddhist approach, we don't relate with art purely as aesthetics, but we approach artistic talent and perception simply, as natural phenomena.

It's a question of paying more attention to the space that exists around us. In doing so, we develop a sense of confidence, confidence that space exists in front of our eyes and that it is not demanding anything. It's a free world, a truly free world. Obviously, in handling our life, questions and hesitations come up constantly. They are like the blank sheet of paper, the canvas. Out of those hesitations, we begin to make a move. We may begin to create a painting or a picture out of that. We are constantly creating and recreating; each moment we are shifting from the previously created picture to creating the next picture. That has something to do with confidence. You have to be extremely sensitive and awake. That is the closest word I can think of: *awake.* Some kind of deliberateness is also necessary. But deliberateness does not mean trying to insert your personal ego; it is purely experiential and inspirational.

Generally, we are extremely keen on becoming artistic, but that is obviously a hang-up. Once we become "artistic," we have a tendency to organize, and to build up dogma around that, and to defend our territory. As soon as we begin to do that, we come up with all kinds of problems: problems of communication with ourselves and problems of communication with others.

Some artists appreciate eccentricity: "He or she is unapproachable, just a crazy artist. Period. That's all." If people try to approach such an artist, he won't speak to them. He only has a few carefully selected friends. He or she won't speak to anybody who does not buy in to his particular trip his particular ego. That kind of approach is well known, and since it amounts to what's known in spirituality as spiritual materialism, we could call it artistic materialism.

Eagerness can be a problem for an artist. When you are eager to do something, you don't perceive the blank sheet of paper or blank canvas in front of you at all. The whole picture is already painted and printed. So you have nothing to paint, nothing to go beyond, nothing further to create. Your vision is completely lopsided—nonexistent, for that matter. You might make something up out of necessity, out of some expectation that you or your friends might have. But the product will be junk. I think *dogshit* is the closest word for it.

Some people may be inspired by violent art, such as pictures of you exploding your head or your brain. But the only people who will be really interested are those with a militant outlook. Although such violent artwork might be presented in a fantastic Zen-like, peaceful fashion, it is absolutely black. You are creating black magic, which harms people rather than helps them. So you should be very careful. Creating a work of art is not a harmless thing. It always is a powerful medium. Art is extraordinarily powerful and important. It challenges people's lives. So there are two choices: either you create black magic to turn people's heads, or you create some kind of basic sanity. Those are the two possibilities, so you should be very, very careful.

Art in Everyday Life

Awareness practice is not just sitting meditation or meditation in action alone.
It is a unique training practice in how to behave as an inspired human being.
That is what is meant by being an artist.

In awareness practice, called *vipashyana* in Sanskrit, there seems to be a need for a general sense of appreciation or artfulness. Awareness practice is highly psychological: it brings a lot of new material into our lives as well as utilizing the material we already have. We could say that an appreciation of mind brings an appreciation of everyday life. So we find that we are surrounded by all kinds of ways of experiencing and expressing our artistic talent, so to speak.

There is a difference between a mindfulness [Skt: *shamatha*] approach to art and an awareness [Skt: *vipashyana*] approach to art. In the case of mindfulness, there is a sense of duty and restriction; a demand is made on us to develop acute, precise mindfulness. Although the tension of being mindful may be very light—we are just touching the verge of the breathing process and there is a sense of freedom—nevertheless, it is still a demand we place on ourselves. In the case of awareness experience, there is simply appreciation. Nothing is hassling us or demanding anything from us. Instead, by means of awareness practice, we could simply tune in to the phenomenal world both inwardly and outwardly.

The idea of the artist is very important and seems to be necessary at this point. When we talk about art, we could be referring to somebody deliberately expressing the beauty and delightfulness or the mockery and crudeness of the world that we live in, in the form of poetry, pictures, or music. That kind of art could be said to be somewhat deliberate art. It is not so much for yourself, but it is more an exhibition, however honest and genuine the artist may be. Such an artist may say that he simply composed his poem because he

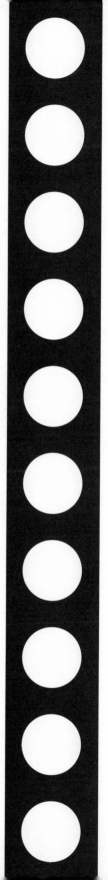

felt that way. But if that's the case, why should he write it down on a piece of paper and date it? If it's just purely for himself, it does not need to be recorded. Whenever a need for recording your work of art is involved, then there is a tendency toward awareness of oneself: "If I record that brilliant idea I've developed, in turn, quite possibly accidentally, somebody might happen to see it and think good of it." There's that little touch involved, however honest and genuine it may be.

A work of art from that point of view is exhibition. I'm not saying that is wrong—by no means. In fact, if we develop a moralistic approach toward art, the whole thing becomes heavy-handed. We try to save ourselves from ego-tripping and just show an inch or a corner of our work of art, afraid that if we do the whole thing completely, we might be indulging our ego and our pride, and so forth. In that approach, there's a lot of hesitation, a pulling back and forth involved. In exhibitionistic art, until you begin to realize that the discipline and training you have received is your possession and you can do what you like with it, until you have that sense of ownership, you will be regarded as halfhearted. That goes with any kind of artwork. The training and discipline you have received is completely inherent; you possess it completely and thoroughly, and it's now up to you how you present it. It's the same as the wisdom of the lineage, which is handed down to a particular lineage holder, and that lineage holder exercises his own authority as to how to present it to his particular generation.

In the practical art of brushstroke paintings, you might assume the painters are free and they can do what they want. The paintings are just blobs of ink put together, and it seems to be coincidental that they make some sense. But those brush painters had long, painful training at the beginning, all of them, in a very orthodox style. In that conservative approach, once the training is completed, then you can do what you want. So even the work of a seemingly free-style person has its root in that conservative interpretation. I think that the tradition of the East has always been of that nature. But in the West, particularly in the twentieth century, people don't always go through a thorough training process first. They purely use their talent, imitating the free style of trained people. And that's very chancy—sometimes they hit and make a tremendous success and sometimes they miss, and the whole thing becomes a tremendous mess. So in order to develop a really free-style work of art, you have to have the awkwardness of seeing yourself being awkward. That kind of watcher seems to be necessary, actually. We have no other choice. The only thing that makes things less serious is to have some kind of humor about the whole thing—not rebellious humor, but appreciating the games that are going on. And that creates further improvisation in brushing one's teeth, or whatever.

Generally, the Tibetan approach is very conservative. Also, the cultural attitude is that there is no secular art in Tibet. If you're going to paint even a free-style thangka, the subject has to be a religious one: different gurus, different deities, or different protectors. So in Tibet you can't have too much of a free hand; whereas in the Zen tradition of China and Japan, often people depict secular art in the language of Zen. As far as social psychology is concerned, their pattern of thinking was much superior to the Tibetans. They didn't stick very faithfully to the doctrine, but they found a way of expressing the teachings in secular art, which seems to have different cultural implications.

The art of meditative experience might be called genuine art. Such art is not designed for exhibition or broadcast. Instead, it is a perpetually growing process in which we begin to appreciate our surroundings in life, whatever they may be—it doesn't necessarily have to be good, beautiful, and pleasurable at all. The definition of art, from this point of view, is to be able to see the uniqueness of everyday experience. Every moment we might be doing the same things—brushing our teeth every day, combing our hair every day, cooking our dinner every day. But that seeming repetitivenes becomes unique every day. A kind of intimacy takes place with the daily habits that you go through and the art involved in it. That's why it is called art in everyday life.

In this country there are many traditions and schools of thought in regard to awareness practice. Attempts are made to develop awareness through awareness of body, awareness of surroundings, and also through encounter groups of various kinds. Those could also be included as works of art. But there's a problem if we are unable to relate with and appreciate the insignificant details of our everyday life. Doing special body awareness practices devoid of everyday life—going to class and doing your thing and coming back—might seem extraordinarily fruitful and liberating; nevertheless, there's still a dichotomy in your life. You feel the importance and the seriousness of the artwork or awareness practice in which you're involved, but, in fact, the more you feel that the whole thing is important and serious, the more your development of awareness is going to be destroyed. Real awareness cannot develop if you are trying to chop your experience into categories and put it into pigeonholes.

One of the things we should overcome in order to become a genuine artist is aggression. The attitude of aggression is one where everything's the same, so what's the difference? It brings with it an outlook on life that the whole world is involved in a plot against you and there's no point even attempting to make it workable. There's no point being involved in details. Everything is the same, so what? It's the attitude of a street fighter. That attitude of aggression is the seed of crudeness, as opposed to artistry. Such crudeness is extremely dumb and blind and misses most of the subtleties of life and its interesting points. If we begin to see even a part of that, the attitude of aggression deliberately shuts us down. That attitude of aggression brings with it the idea of the needlessness of being meticulous or of repetitive effort in trying to relate with things. If you are not able to see a particular situation clearly the first time, you might go back a second time and third time and fourth time—but aggression kills that potential of going back and developing the patience actually to experience it. So we could quite safely categorize aggression and impatience as anti-art, the source of crudeness.

In the awareness experience, you are able to see the shadow of your watcher by being patient. You do not want to get hold of just one chunk of mindfulness and stick with it, but you experience the mindfulness *and* its shadow, the environment around it. There is a tremendous appreciation of life and of how to conduct one's life. So awareness practice is not just formal sitting meditation or meditation in action alone. It is a unique training practice in how to behave as an inspired human being, or inspired sentient being. That is what is meant by being an artist.

While other artists take a deliberately artistic or exhibitionistic approach, with awareness practice your entire ability and all your potentials are completely opened. (I'm not using the term *exhibitionistic* pejoratively, but in a neutral way.) You don't need very much inspiration at all. Actually, you don't need that much vocabularay or tricks of any kind to create good works of art—poetry, painting, music, or whatever. You just simply say the experience you've experienced—just say it, just play it, just paint it. Once you've begun to break that kind of backwater, there are gushes of all kinds of energies. And since the first attempt was free and clear and resourceful, then the second and third and fourth creations of art are no problem at all. It comes naturally, quite simply. However, if you are concerned, thinking, "Oh, I can't write poetry; I've never done it. I used to do it in school, but I was a rather bad one. I can't even draw a circle. I can't even sing"—that is simply hesitation. This has nothing to do with artistic talent. Professional, mechanical talent is not the obstacle—it is the psychological aggression that has to be worked on. When that psychological aggression is transmuted into the energy of artistic talent, you begin to realize that you can do all kinds of things—to your amazement.

There are a lot of implications of art in vipashyana experience, not only for painting and other artistic media, but also for relationships generally— how to communicate, how to speak, how to cook, how to choose one's clothes in a shop, how to select food at the supermarket—all those little details. Some people get extremely paranoid because they weren't brought up in cultured society, so to speak, and did not have any opportunities for learning how to go about such things. People become paranoid, aggressive, and "hufty-pufty" and come down on gentility as just being another trip: "I don't have to do that, I'm quite happy with my crudeness." But again, the aggression is the problem. It is not that you have to tune in to special information or a certain tradition, a particular style of eating, a particular style of dressing. This has nothing to do with a particular culture; rather, it has something to do with your instinct—that your instinct is open and has the room to exercise its potentialities into action. Then, for the very fact of being a genteel animal, human beings bring out their own man-animal-like, apelike, or genteel-ape tastes, whatever comes through.

Particularly in this country, the present conventional art is concentrated on the mere representation of sarcasm and crudeness, and it is ultimately unbearable, ugly, dirty—and thought provoking, no doubt. It seems that artists find it comfortable to produce that kind of art, because they are afraid to put a positive message out to the masses. Any positive messages they might have are a problem. The safest way of putting out some kind of artistic message is to do so from the angle of criticizing the existing flow of society, which is very safe. That might be said to be the same trick as Nagarjuna's logic, which is that one should not dwell on anything, one should not have any philosophy at all. If we don't have any philosophy, we are safe, and we could criticize the nihilist and the eternalist and even those who dwell in the middle—and that's our philosophy. But somehow there's something not quite straightforward about that. After all, as Buddhists, we are followers of the Buddha, the Maharishi, the Great Rishi who followed the straightforward path. Likewise, in art, it seems to be necessary and important that we create a target of ourselves. We may become a target of criticism by presenting positive art, but that might be the best approach. It is the same thing in our daily life: not negating everything that happens in our lives, negation being a lifestyle, but getting into and presenting certain positive steps, like an appreciation of beauty. So art in the transcendental sense becomes the real practice of awareness, or vipashyana.

In the past we have talked about becoming good students of a tea maker, learning how to make a perfect cup of tea and how to entertain friends. From the ordinary way of looking, that seems to be just like parents' wishes that their children grow up and become society boys and society girls—that you entertain your friends ideally and occupy them and say the right things at the right moment, and everything runs smoothly. But in this case, it's much more than that. If you link that with the idea of awareness practice, then it is becoming a bodhisattva, which is the highest, most supreme society person that we could ever imagine. The bodhisattva is known as the great host, the ship, the bridge, the highway, the mountain, the earth—all of which deal with interactions with people. So there is a lot of potential in us. And that element could be applied at the beginning level of vipashyana practice as well; we don't have to start on such a big scale. Our energy and money and space and experience may be limited, but at least we can start on the practical level of developing an awareness of that potential.

We can start with the possibility of vipashyana experience, which is that everyday life is a work of art if you see it from a point of view of nonaggression. That point is extremely important, particularly in order to overcome clumsiness and crudeness, which in this case is not ordinary clumsiness and crudeness, but fundamental, phenomenological clumsiness and crudeness. Aggression is anti-art. If you are not in an aggressive state of mind, you feel you are rich and resourceful and infinitely inspired. When somebody is angry and uptight—even such ordinary, literal aggression as anger—then it cuts all possibilities of improvising what exists in your life as part of your artistic talent. It is not there anymore, because if things potentially improvisable come up, you become angry at them and they become a nuisance. You would like to kick them out, destroy them. It is like an angry person who comes home and, not finding a way to express his anger, starts throwing chairs and hitting the table. That is a very unartistic thing to do and, to say the least, rather pathetic.

At the same time, anger and aggression are different. If you relate with your anger in such a way that it also inspires a work of poetry, there must be some generosity involved, or at least some kind of awareness. So art is not just creating beauty; it is anything workable and rich. And as far as art in everyday life and the awareness experience is concerned, transcending aggression is the root of all the artistic talent one can ever imagine.

Ordinary Truth

There is symbolism when you wake up, when you feel dirty and wish you could take a shower, when you take your shower and feel refreshed, when you feel hungry, when you eat your breakfast, bacon and eggs sunny-side up, toast and marmalade, quite possibly a waffle or pancakes, and when you are willing to face the day after a hearty breakfast and coffee. That is all symbolism.

People's usual idea of symbolism is that it is something outside them, like a signpost or billboard, that gives them signs, perhaps of religious significance. That's not quite true. Symbolism is connected with your self, your inner being. In other words, you are the biggest symbol of yourself. That is symbolism. Often you don't want to listen to yourself talking on tape, and if you see photographs that have been taken of you, you get embarrassed. You think they could be better, and you don't want to see what you look like from somebody else's point of view. But maybe you should look into that more. You are a caricature of yourself and a symbol of yourself. Everything is its own caricature, by itself. That is symbolism on its own, the symbolism of experience itself. For instance, when you create a visual symbol, first it presents itself. Ideas come afterward. That's the whole point. If you do interior decoration in a room, it speaks for itself. Later, people may get conceptual or metaphysical feelings about it. So everything stands by itself, and as far as you are concerned, you are a symbol of yourself. Symbolism is based on what we experience personally and directly in our lives: pain, pleasure, or whatever. From that point of view, symbolism is a state of mind.

First of all, before we know anything about anything, we have problems with motivation. If we view the whole world as raw material, like a simple sheet of canvas, a simple piece of wood, or a simple piece of clay, what is its relationship with ourselves? That piece of canvas or clay, being an inanimate object, has no particular personal interest or desire to form itself into a painting or a sculpture. But as human beings, we *do* have ideas about how our life should be, how our understanding should take place. So we are caught in a double bind: we want to understand, but we would also like to reshape the universe according to our own expectations.

There are two basic understandings of symbolism: the theistic and the nontheistic. Theistic symbolism is a constant self-existing confirmation; that is, whenever symbolism exists, you exist and your world exists. In the case of a nontheistic symbolism such as Buddhism, you don't exist, symbolism doesn't exist, and the universe doesn't exist. That's quite shocking! "How do we go beyond that?" you might ask. But we don't actually go beyond that. Instead of trying to go beyond it, we try to get into it.

The basic notion of nontheistic symbolism is that whatever exists in our life—our birth, our death, our sickness, our marriage, our business adventure, our educational adventure—is based on symbolism of some kind. This type of symbolism may not be the vivid visions you see by tuning your system in to a mystical state of mind, such as fantastic auras with symbols in the middle. In fact, from the point of view of nontheism, such perceptions are regarded as bullshit. Maybe you need more rest or another cup of coffee. We do not go along with any kind of highfalutin colorful adventures, cosmic explosions of color after color, or fantastic visions. Looking for magical messages, as opposed to a direct relationship, creates a barrier to understanding symbolism.

In the nontheistic discipline of Buddhism, we do not glorify *that* because we want to confirm *this*. Instead, we simply go along. We are not denying God, but we are simply trying to approach reality as simply as we could. A tortoise walks and carries a heavy shell; a cow walks along and grazes by itself in a green meadow, depositing its dung; pigeons make their own noises and live on the roof. Things have their own place. They don't have to be commanded by the higher or the greater, particularly. Things are as they are, ordinary and simple. Seemingly, that is a very simpleminded approach, but actually it is extremely deep.

Symbolism usually comes as messages. It is a very simple eye-level relationship: me and my world. You could forget the sky, or the It, Him, or Her. That makes the whole thing extremely simple: there's no Big Brother watching you. Symbols of all kinds occur throughout our life, and whether you believe it or not, the most penetrating and powerful symbol in our life is pain. Therefore, the symbolism of suffering is very important and realistic. Complaints occur *right here*—not up there or down below, but in the middle, where we are living, where we are actually experiencing our life on this particular earth. We are not underground, and we are not up in the air—even though people get fascinated that Tibetans can levitate. In fact, there was one eccentric old gentleman in England who wrote me and said that he wanted to start a laboratory of Tibetans levitating behind glass, but his plan didn't come off.

Basic suffering is very powerful ground, and the basis of man's attitude toward symbolism. The only immediate symbolism we can experience is pain. It is the direct message that we have been constantly involved in seeking pleasure of all kinds—and when the search for pleasure becomes our theme, that automatically provides a reference point to pain. We may feel relatively good, with nothing to complain about, particularly. But then we would like to entertain ourselves more. We go to the movies, but the movie is terrible, so we decide to go to a restaurant, but the food isn't so good—or, for that matter, we go and see a great movie and have a fantastic meal in a restaurant! *All of that* is an expression of basic pain.

The existence in our mind of basic pain is extremely powerful and difficult to shake off. Basically, we feel captured by our life. We can't get out of it; we are stuck with it. We don't want to get into it—maybe it is too much for us. So we are stuck in the middle of it all the time. We may try to blame our pain on the past, but what we are experiencing is in the present, here and now. Even if our pain did develop in the past, it is impossible to change that. We are stuck with our regular thinking, our regular world as it is. We have to take what we are given. It's our world, whether we like it or not. As they say, "America—love it or leave it." That's great symbolism. The American flag: you can't take it, you can't leave it, it's always there.

Pain takes place all the time, and pleasure takes place all the time. The problem is that we really don't want to relate with the actuality of things as they are. We don't want to relate with that kind of symbolism, but it is always there. You have to share the meaning of symbolism personally, the pain and pleasure aspect of symbolism, definitely so. Otherwise, we cannot discuss the meaning of symbolism; we have nothing to talk about. That basic symbolism of pain and its hang-ups pervades our entire life. There is symbolism when you wake up, when you feel dirty and wish you could take a shower, when you take your shower and feel refreshed, when you feel hungry, when you eat your breakfast, bacon and eggs sunny-side up, toast and marmalade, quite possibly a waffle or pancakes, and when you are willing to face the world after a hearty breakfast and coffee. That is all symbolism. The idea of coffee, and in fact the word *coffee,* is very provocative. It is mantra. *Pancakes, eggs, bacon.* That is all extremely powerful, very poetic, although we don't want to get into any trip about being a poet. Everything that goes on in our life is related with some kind of symbolism.

Our simple daily life could be involved with that kind of statement all the time, but we reject it as a purely mundane thing. We regard it as a terrible hassle and forget the whole thing. We drink our coffee and eat our bacon and eggs, just to get it over with. Then we go to the meditation hall and sit on a cushion and think maybe that will be a big thing for us. Somehow symbolism doesn't work that way. The basic point of tantra is interest and awareness in every activity we are involved in throughout our life, at every moment.

There is always some kind of message taking place. What message? We don't know. It's up to you. There's not going to be a fantastic dictionary or encyclopedia. This is simply a reminder that every activity you are doing — smoking cigarettes, chewing gum — has some kind of meaning behind it. The simple point is that the things you do shouldn't be missed. You should experience what you do. (But don't be heavy-handed, as if you were going to write a book about it. I don't want to make this into a trip.)

At every moment, our every move usually has a thought-provoking quality. The universe is constantly trying to reach us to say something or teach something, but we are rejecting it all the time. In categorizing your experience as mundane and sacred, good and bad, significant and insignificant, you are rejecting symbolism, right and left, all the time. You are rejecting the whole thing. By fitting everything into categories and pigeonholes, you have nothing left in your life except your own pain. But this pain is not really productive pain, like the original basic pain we were talking about. Instead, you just rot yourself into a grain of sand. That is not really very romantic. It's a terrible thing. Finally it is as if your ingrown toenail becomes monstrous and eats you up, not only your toe but your whole body and your expansive, energetic vision. Everything is disheveled.

The basic point is that we have very many possibilities of symbolism: every activity taking place is basic symbolism. I would like you actually to appreciate the world around you and begin to understand the facts and figures, the basic realities. There are a lot of things taking place. Symbolism doesn't have to be poetic or spiritual or mystical; it is the ordinary truth that takes place in everyday life. Buddhist symbolism is both unique in its nontheistic approach and very ordinary. Altogether, it is simply our living situation—life and experience, life and experience—very simple and direct.

Empty Gap of Mind

In order to realize unconditional symbolism, we have to appreciate the empty gap of our state of mind and how we begin to project ourselves into that non—reference point.

Unless we have some basic understanding of the foundations of Buddhist psychology, we have no way of understanding symbolism at all. So we are preparing our ground with integrity and at a slow pace. We do not want to present tantric symbolism California-style. Instead, we will go slowly, step by step.

Symbolism has to do with phenomenal experience, the various realms of phenomena that can be experienced through the five sense perceptions, particularly the very powerful auditory and visual perceptions. Phenomena as traditionally known are inspired purely by the five sense perceptions. We also try to piece phenomena together, to record and edit them in our mind, which in Buddhism is considered a sixth sense. For instance, if as a child we were slapped by a parent, that particular phenomenon is recorded in our mind; so the next time we are tempted to do the same thing, it is quite clear what will happen to us—we will be slapped again. That's sort of an adolescent phenomenal experience in which a reference point, or relationship, takes place. There seem to be further phenomena as we grow up and go to school, and we are told all sorts of facts and figures and stories. We begin to build our phenomenal experience further, into possibilities of all kinds: how we relate with other children, exchange information back and forth, watch Sesame Street, or whatever it may be. In all these details, phenomenal experience is shared.

As we grow further, we begin to relate with philosophy and spirituality, whatever our particular approach may be. Our phenomenal experience becomes much more complicated, not that childhood phenomenal experience is all that simple. Some underlying unsaid communication takes place all the time, and the phenomenal world becomes extremely complicated and tiresome

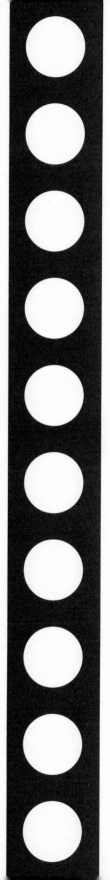

sometimes. Other times, we simply can't live without it. We have to have phenomenal experiences of all kinds. If we don't have enough ordinary phenomenal experiences, we go out and buy newspapers, watch television, go to the movies, or even take trips to foreign countries to see how other people live, which are superphenomena.

At the beginning, as we are growing up, the phenomenal world is simply based on survival and our need to communicate with our living situation. In order to ask our mother to cook an egg, soup, or cereal, we have to have some symbolism in mind: we think *soup, egg,* or *cereal.* At first we don't actually say it properly, but we think it. We visualize it fully and completely. Then we utter the word *egg, soup,* or *cereal.* When we vomit out those words, our parents are very proud of us, because we are beginning to talk and to communicate. Perceiving symbolism—relating with any kind of symbolism in the world—is based on that growth of phenomenal experience. It projects outward personally at all levels: at the grownup, old-age, youngster, teenager, and infant levels, such phenomenal experiences take place constantly. We could classify those phenomenal experiences as symbolism, definitely, but it is relative symbolism rather than absolute symbolism.

It is important to realize that those little phenomenal experiences are produced by restlessness, by searching for further entertainment, by looking into and investigating our world. What is the world made out of? What is the world, anyway? We ask all kinds of questions of our parents, professors, friends, elders, uncles, aunts, psychiatrists. We are trying to sort out what this world is. We want so badly to find out what it is all about. Some people think they have some kind of clue, possibilities of that and this. But we are still depending on the possibility of finding *the answer,* and in that sense, we are all babies. This has nothing to do with chronological age. We simply do not have enough experience of symbolism or the realization of what symbolism means, so whether we are old or young, we are still like infants. That seems to be a problem—or maybe a promise.

In order to understand absolute symbolism, we first have to get squared with the relative phenomenal world, or relative symbolism. So try to understand this point. At this moment, how we view our world personally is not very difficult; but at the same time, it is extraordinarily difficult and complicated. We would like to have access to our particular world at this very moment, as though it were a gigantic baby bottle and we could take a sip. We want to be fed all the time, to suck rather than just sit. That is a crude way of putting it, but it is not meant to undermine your individual dignity. I respect your dignity and splendor, but let's face it—everybody wants to be a big baby. Some of us are bold and hungry enough that we would like the whole bottle in our mouth, with a huge nipple. Some people are more polite and don't want a big bottle, which would make them very self-conscious, so they have a little thin tube. Apart from political and social concerns, the whole thing boils down to the fact that we are big babies, quite lovable ones.

When you begin to understand relative symbolism, you realize that relative symbolism is like a nipple. You are fed constantly. If you are restless or uptight, you can suck violently; if you are angry, you could bite it. We are stuck with that big nipple, big bank of comfort, all the time. It is smothering. Relative symbolism is based on passion, which also means restlessness, demandingness, and aggression. We are fed with spiritual fluid, or temporary domestic fluid, in connection with our perceptions of the world and how we feel. And since the definition of dharma, according to the Buddhist tradition, is passionlessness, relative symbolism is not real dharma.

At this point, I would like to shift our attitude from being big babies and discuss absolute symbolism. I hope you are up to it. Absolute symbolism is not a dream world at all, but realistic. As far as linguistics is concerned, *absolute* means "needing no reference point." Otherwise, absolute would become relative, because it would have a relationship with something else. So absolute is free from reference point. It is wholesome, complete by itself, self-existing.

The idea of absolute symbolism is also passionless and egoless. How come? Actually, as far as absolute is concerned, you don't come but you go. It is a going process rather than a coming process, not a collector's mentality, in which you store everything in your big bank with fat money behind it, or your big bottle. Absolute symbolism is egoless, because you have already abandoned your psychological reference point. That doesn't mean you have abandoned your parents, or your body, or anything of that nature. So what is that reference point? It is a sense of reassurance that makes you feel better. It's like when you are crying and your friends come along and hold you and say, "Don't cry, everything's going to be okay. There's nothing to worry about. We'll take care of you. Take a sip of milk. Let's take a walk in the woods, have a drink together." That type of psychological reference point is based on the idea of relative truth.

The absolute truth of egolessness does not need any of those comforts. But that is actually a very dangerous thing to mention at this point. I have my reservations as to whether I should talk about these things, and since I have lost my boss, I have no one to talk to. So I decided to go ahead and tell you. A sense of empty-heartedness takes place when we lose our reference point. If you do not have any reference point at all, you have nothing to work with, nothing to compare with, nothing to fight, nothing to try to subtract or add into your system at all. You find yourself absolutely nowhere, just empty heart, big hole in your brain. Your nervous system doesn't connect with anything, and there's no logic particularly, just empty heart. That empty-heartedness could be regarded in some circles as an attack of the evil ones and in other circles as an experience of *satori,* or sudden enlightenment.

People actually have no idea what non-reference-point experience is. When you begin to abandon all possibilities of any kind of reference point that would comfort you, tell you to do something, help you to see through everything, make you a better and greater person—when you lose all those reference points, including your ambition, the strangest thing takes place. Usually people think that if you lose everything—your ambition, your self-centeredness, your integrity and dignities—you will become a vegetable, a jellyfish. But it's not so. You don't become a jellyfish. Instead, you are suspended in space, in a big hole of some kind. It is quite titillating. Big hole of suspension! It's as if you were suspended in outer space without a space suit or rocket ship. You are just floating and circulating around the planets forever and ever.

That sense of suspension is the ground, according to the non-reference-point view of how to perceive absolute symbolism. That experience of suspension is the canvas or the blackboard where you paint your pictures, your symbolism. It is the basic ground. You can only begin from there. It is the empty stage you can perform on. I'm not saying that you flip into that state of mind, and you are stuck with that particular experience for the rest of your life, necessarily. But we do have such a state of mind; such an experience occurs all the time. Throughout our life there are occasional experiences of this black hole, suspended space, where we have no reference point. No matter how much we kick, how hard we try to push, how hard we breathe, we don't get anywhere. We're just suspended in a vacuum. Such an experience takes place with everybody, all the time. But nobody has realized that from that experience you can cultivate your potential artistic talent, your dharma art visual appreciation, and begin to experience symbolism altogether. That idea has occurred to very few people. It has only occurred to our grandparents, the holders of the lineage, the people who made the symbols and experienced the symbols personally. They actually executed them, so this is not so much doctrine as the personal experience of our grandparents and great-great-grandparents, who experienced that black hole frequently. Out of that black hole of egolessness and no-discursive-thought, a color occurred, a symbol occurred, or a fraction of a symbol occurred.

Traditionally speaking, a symbol occurs because a symbol is unborn, unceasing, and its nature is like the sky, like space. Those are the three principles of absolute symbolism. *Unborn* means that symbolism cannot happen if there is no place to give birth to symbolism. Space can give birth to symbolism, because symbolism did not exist and does not exist. Because of its nonexistence, there is immense energy and power to create an image of nonexistence. So images of immense power and immense clarity, sharp-edged and crystal clear, take place. *Unceasing* means that symbolism cannot die once it has been given birth to within the level of nonexistence. Symbolism cannot die; it remains in the hearts of all human beings—all sentient beings, in fact. Symbolism is everlasting, but nobody has to nurture it, nurse it, or hold on to it. Third, since its nature is like the sky, like space, people can execute such symbolism from their own experience, their own perception. So giving birth to absolute symbolism requires no-mind, which is big mind, great mind. This may sound like complete gibberish, but it makes a lot of sense. The idea of nonexistence also being highly existent, eternally existing, is very tricky. It is a very powerful statement.

In that projection into space, there are no materials, no constituents out

41

of which to make your symbols. For instance, you might be watching a dead dog, and that whole perception is an experience of nothing happening. We are not talking about the psychological functioning of a holy man, an enlightened person, or a buddha. We are talking about our own perceptions: we can experience this too, it's right here, we could do it. When you experience a dead dog bleeding, its teeth showing and somewhat dirty, its fur covered with dust, and its innards slowly coming out, skin torn, and blood running onto the ground—if you look at it from a conceptual point of view, it's a terrible idea. It's not artistic to talk about such a terrible subject. I am certain we shouldn't talk about such things; we are too genteel to talk about such dirty things. You mustn't even mention death or blood; you only do that when you swear. However, it is blank mind that projects the vision of a dead dog lying on the ground. It may be revolting, and sometimes interestingly colorful, expecting possibilities of the future. Nevertheless, behind that whole thing there is a space of nothing actually happening, because you are so shocked.

We can look at a beautiful rose with its gentle petals, velvetlike, but not as rough as velvet. It is so delicate and beautiful, like an infant's tongue. It is fantastically fresh and beautiful and sends out its fragrance. We could see little tears sitting all over it, the dew of the morning slowly melting and finally becoming an adornment of that particular rose flower. An occasional breeze sways it back and forth and gives it a sense of being alive. A beautiful rose flower. You are so fascinated, so appreciative of that particular image. In looking at that rose, there is exactly the same perspective of empty mind that takes place in watching the dead dog.

Although I'm sure you don't really want to associate those two things— one is horrible and one is so beautiful—you are still doing the same thing all the time. If you watch a beautiful rose or if you watch a dead dog bleeding with its innards out, the same experience of blankness takes place. That is where symbolism actually begins to occur in your state of mind. When you first perceive something, there is a shock of no conceptual mind operating at all. Then something begins to occur. You begin to perceive: whether you like it or not, you begin to see colors and perceptions, to open your eyes. So that non-reference-point mind can become highly powerful and extraordinarily sensitive.

That is an interesting point of view, and it can be conducted in ordinary human situations. For instance, my own students like to find out where things are going wrong. They have lots of complaints—very intelligent complaints, not just ordinary complaints. Because of that, their intelligence begins to heighten, so that their complaints do not become real complaints but an expression of clarity, or clear-mindedness. So we are not talking about the perceptions of the Buddha, the *arhats,* the bodhisattvas, or the great tantric masters. We are talking about the principles of perception. In order to realize unconditional symbolism, we have to appreciate the empty gap of our state of mind and how we begin to project ourselves into that non—reference point.

Coloring Our World

If we are to be able to perceive symbolism, we have to abandon this *so that we become completely with* that *— the events of life, the expressions of life, the colorful play of life. That seems to be the basic point.*

In our lives, there is a lot of symbolism, or reminders, so to speak. Sometimes we miss them, and sometimes we experience them. And when we experience them, sometimes we experience them incorrectly and sometimes correctly. It seems to depend on the dogma of the situation, which leads us to the topic of obstacles to realizing symbolism.

An important obstacle to experiencing symbolism is expectations. We have been brought up with all kinds of reference points and frameworks of ideas, which we use to try to recapture the crucial experiences that highlight our lives. For instance, we would like to recapture our lover by identifying our lover with some symbol, concept, or connotation. And we would like to relate with our parents, our sisters and brothers, and our friends in this same way. In a constant attempt to make our lives worthwhile, we try to make each thing that comes up into a highlight, the best possible situation. It could be the time we spent in the hospital, the time somebody told us about some person, the time we had with our teacher in school, whatever. We make these things into very interesting highlights—but in doing so we are missing the point of symbolism.

We experience some shift or breakthrough in our minds in *every* situation, whether it is an experience induced by psychedelic drugs or a natural experience such as a personal dilemma, personal revelation, or personal tragedy. Then we turn *some* of these experiences into highlights. And often, one particular highlight becomes a crucial password in our lives, a turning point. "The first time I had that experience I felt fantastic! It struck me like a bolt from the blue!" But whether an experience is ordinary or extraordinary, *every* experience is regarded as a message. It is not like a telegram from Western Union, announcing that somebody died or got married; it is a message of the natural situation. Since it is a natural message, therefore we decided to call it symbolism.

In relating to natural symbolism, the fault arises from your sense of personal expectations. You would like to see yourself playing a certain role in society—or within yourself, for that matter. You would like to be such and such a person, playing such and such a role. Of course, you could easily say that you do not have any expectations. But the desire not to have expectations only becomes another form of expectation. In fact, that is a great expectation, because you begin to feel that not having expectations is the best way to attain your expectations. So expectations are a stumbling block. We color and re-edit our experiences drastically. How do we do that? We do it with our passion, aggression, and ignorance.

Passion colors our expectations with desire. We see whatever is connected to us in terms of warmth, friendliness, and congeniality. We are constantly trying to mold our expectations in terms of what we want. The rest of what we hear is completely inaudible; the rest of what we see is completely invisible. We only take in what we want to see and hear. Expectations also take the form of aggression, or rejecting. Whatever we see or hear is constantly subject to our rejection. We would like to push away anything presented to us as either logically or personally inapplicable. We reject all those facts and figures, so we can't hear and we can't see. Another form of expectation is known as ignorance, according to traditional Buddhist language. Here this is a sense of basic panic, basic bewilderment, basic pain. We are completely numbed by the situation, so we can't hear or see. We can't even reject or accept. Instead, whenever a situation does not suit our requirements, we automatically create a mental block to shut it off. We are confused and terrified by all those uncertainties.

These three types of experience—passion, aggression, and ignorance—occur in our minds because behind all that there is a governing factor, which is our belief in "I," "me." "Me" or "I" is not very visionary: it's very personal, very domestic, and very petty. "I" would like to do certain things. "I" would like to experience certain things. Whenever that word *I* flashes in our mind, our experience is that we are willing to employ any one of those three convenient tactics: passion, aggression, or ignorance. We are willing to employ any of those possible tactics so that "I" can be preserved. In that way, "I" cannot be challenged; "I" cannot be manipulated by such undesirable situations as the nonexistence of "I" or the possibility of giving up territory altogether. That is the general problem that takes place. Whenever there is the word "I," "me," or "I am," there is a sense of *thisness,* which is extremely strong. Therefore, our sense of *thatness* has to be conditioned by whatever is experienced by *this.* So we begin to have problems with *that.* We try to reject it, which is an expression of aggression; we try to magnetize it or suck it in, which is an expression of passion; or we ignore the whole thing, which is an expression of ignorance. Since expectations relate with passion, aggression, and ignorance, if you could see through their particular games, then the expectations themselves would be transparent. It's a question of clarity, as well as self-confidence.

The experience of I, me, a personal existence, ego, self, whatever you want to call it, has a sense of immense fundamental pain. You don't want to exist, you don't want to be, but you can't help it. Children often complain to their parents: "Why did you bring me into this world! What am I doing here! Who am I?" There is a lot of resentment toward existence; self-existence is a painful point. Sometimes mystical traditions talk about a fantastic rediscovery of self, rediscovering who I am. But if you look at that as purely rediscovering your identity, that mystical experience becomes another push to play spiritual games, I'm afraid.

The fundamental effect of ego and its tricks is becoming hardened. It actually prevents the sensitivity of experiencing the total, complete reality of symbolism. Of course, from the realm of ego, you can manufacture your own little symbolism, your own little messages. But that's just adding to your confusion, rather than seeing absolute symbolism. If we are to be able to perceive symbolism, we have to abandon *this* so that we become completely with *that*—the events of life, the expressions of life, the colorful play of life. That seems to be the basic point.

The source of sophistication that allows us to be able to see messages coming here and there, ordinary symbolism, is some kind of gap—*that* which is free of *this*. Without that, we are unable to experience anything of that nature; everything is "me" all over the place, "I am" all over the place. Whatever you experience is only "me" talking back to you. From that perspective, everything's okay: you could kill somebody, destroy somebody, and actually confuse the whole world as much as you yourself are confused. That is a journey toward making cosmic garbage, rather than cosmic vision. But our intention is not to create further garbage.

Basically, the main obstacle to the perception of symbolism is our ego. We are allergic to ourselves; therefore, we create all kinds of sicknesses and pains. And even when we take our medicine, unless the doctor is completely wise and understanding, the medicine doesn't have any effect on us, because we are allergic to ourselves. People may ask if you are allergic to penicillin or aspirin, but nobody asks, "Are you allergic to yourself?" Nobody's thought of that. If you do not have clear vision or clear perception, it is because you are allergic to yourself. So before you take any medicine to clear up your vision and be able to perceive symbolism, you'd better check on how allergic you are to yourself. You might think about that question for a while. Then you will begin to see what the problem is in experiencing direct communication from what exists in the world. You will begin to see why certain messages don't click and other messages do click; certain things work and certain things don't work.

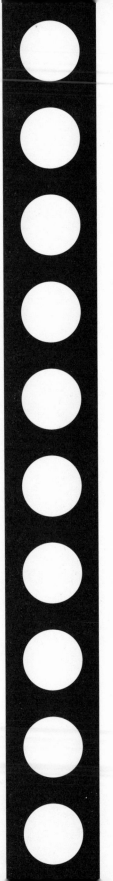

New Sight

Symbolism is a question of gaining new sight. It is being extremely inquisitive to see things in their own nature.

Symbolism is a question of gaining new sight. It is being extremely inquisitive to see things in their own nature, not always wanting to change things. The opposite of symbolic vision is resentment, fear, and too much philosophy. You want to change the whole world. You want to hang the picture upside down, but somehow that doesn't work. The Sheratons, Holiday Inns, delicatessens, and restaurants are still there. It is all still there, completely solid and definite. If you take one attitude toward it, the whole thing is absolutely humorless and rigid. It doesn't mean anything; it's the same bad old life, which gives you shivers in your system. You have had problems all your life dealing with things as they are, which are not so good. But you could take a different attitude, seeing things as they are in their own value, in their own spaciousness.

Basically, what we perceive is a square world that has a ceiling, walls, and floor. It is the same as seeing through a camera lens. There are perspectives of all kinds. To begin with, there is space above—the ceiling or heaven. Some people want to think there is something above the ceiling, called a loft. All sorts of people live up there and conduct business downward. And some people think that there is something behind the wall: your neighbors, cities, highways. Then you have the floor, and maybe downstairs there is a cellar, or the heart of the earth where a lot of hot things are going on. It might explode at any time. That's a possibility someday, I suppose. So we are living in a square world.

Even if we are outside of our house, we still are living in a square world. In this case, when we look up and see the ceiling, it's called the sky. We look around us and see the mountains or buildings. We look down and see streets

Vajradhara. A traditional thangka painting by Sherab Palden.

Reeds. *Chögyam Trungpa Rinpoche.*

Texaco sign. *Chögyam Trungpa Rinpoche.*

Branches. *Chögyam Trungpa Rinpoche.* "We could view the trees as cracks in the sky, like cracks in glasses. We could adopt that change of perspective. The space that exists around you could be solid—and you could be only a hollow in the middle of that solid space."

Wire. *Chögyam Trungpa Rinpoche.*

Beam. *Chögyam Trungpa Rinpoche.* "People keep taking photographs of sunsets, so I thought I might take a photograph of a moonset. It is sort of a vajra shot, the precision of it."

Vidyadhara painting a Guru Rinpoche thangka, Dalhousie, India, 1963.

Spontaneous calligraphy on overhead projector. Los Angeles Dharma Art Seminar.

"Explorers of the Richness of the Phenomonal World" in the Los Angeles Arboretum.

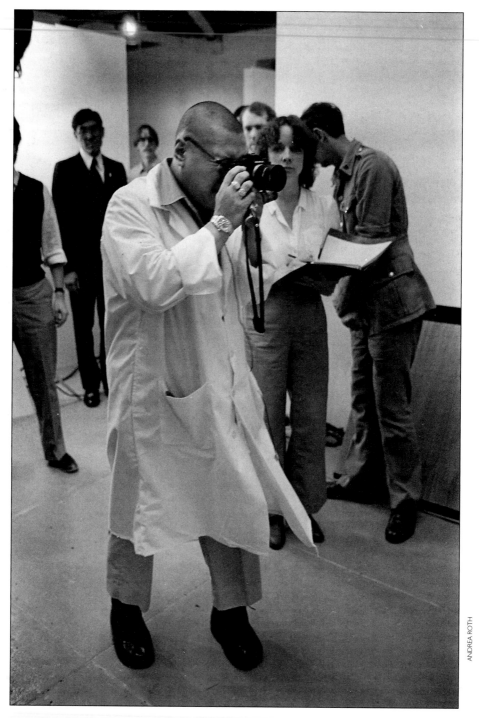

ANDREA ROTH

Shooting photos, Los Angeles Environmental Installation.

Filming. Unknown location.

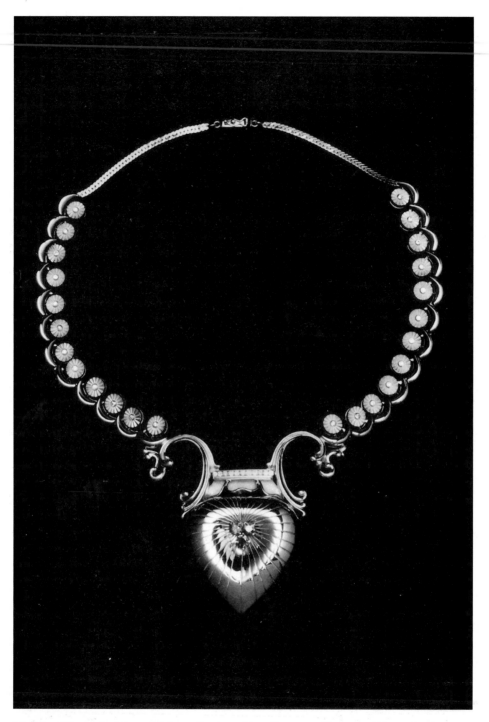

Necklace for Lady Diana Mukpo. Designed by Chögyam Trungpa Rinpoche, in collaboration with Gina Stick.

Spontaneous calligraphy. Dharma Art Seminar, Boulder, Colorado.

Flower exhibit, Denver.

Placing reeds. Flower exhibit, Denver.

Lichen. *Chögyam Trungpa Rinpoche.* "This is a piece of rock with lichen on it. It's another overcrowded, ratna situation, which provides some kind of space at the same time. It's like the view I have of all you people from up here. There are not very many gaps—you almost cover the whole floor, and I regard that as space."

Construction site. *Chögyam Trungpa Rinpoche.* "You might say that this photograph is a typical example of aggression. Everything in the picture goes on
in its own way without admitting any little suggestions, and everything in it is
prefabricated except the grass. Nevertheless, it could also be a point of gentleness.
There are no trips involved in scenery like this. There is natural beauty, natural
sloppiness, and natural chaos."

Formal Garden. Designed by Chögyam Trungpa Rinpoche, in collaboration with
Kanjuro Shibata Sensei. GES Building, Boulder, Colorado.

Library. Los Angeles Environmental Installation.

Garden. Los Angeles Environmental Installation.

or paths. That world is usually what we see. We would like to have somewhere to lean back and take a rest, chairs with backrests and arms we can lean on. Then we have the front, in which we could launch our projects. But we still have the ceiling. We would like to keep a ceiling and a roof both, as shelter from rain, hail, and snowfall. In other words, we are living in a box, and our vision is a box.

Photographs are also boxlike. We have a square camera with a square perspective, and as we wind our film we see one square after another. That squareness seems to be our general frame of reference. But we don't have to be too concerned with that squareness—we could dance with it. Let's view that corner, this corner, this corner and that corner. Above we could allow lots of space; at the bottom we could allow a lot of solidity; on the sides we could play with how we view our world. If the world is pushing us to the left or the right, we could go along with that. As long as we don't fight, there's no problem. We could have the right invading our left; that's okay, that's a nice picture. If the left is invading our right, that also makes a nice picture.

The basic principle of photography from that point of view is viewing things as they are in their own ordinary nature. It is very simple and direct. We should be prepared to see how we can present a picture or concept in our minds. Can we do it or not? The obvious answer is that we can do it. However, we actually should be willing to see a particular vision without expectation or conceptualization. We should have the perspective of being willing to take any kind of good old, bad old shot. The whole point is that we should be extremely careful and inquisitive about what we see in our world: what we see with our eyes, what we actually perceive, both how we see and what we see. This is very important.

There's an old saying, "Seeing's not believing." That's true. When we see something, we don't have to believe in it, but we do have to see it properly. We have to *look* at it—then it might be true. The interesting point here is that in sharpening our perception completely and properly, we don't have to put philosophical or metaphysical jargon into it. We are just dealing precisely and directly with how our perception or vision works as we look at an object and how our mind changes by looking at it.

In discussing symbolism or iconography, we have to consider everything in absolute detail. We have to think slowly, to slow down. It is not so much getting ideas and information as fast as we can, but as *slowly* as we can, so that we have an understanding of the basic setup. For instance, we could examine a very high quality Tibetan thangka executed by a great Tibetan art master. There's blue paint ground from lapis lazuli; white from some kind of chalk; the red is vermilion; the yellow is pure gold; and the green is a kind of vegetable paint. If you take such a thangka and divide it into small sections, you might get some idea as to how things can proceed by paying more attention to details. Everything in that thangka was carefully chosen by an individual person who was actually interested in such works of art. Likewise, we need to see how much effort and understanding we have to put into our lives to live properly and completely. Otherwise, we may have a problem, because we want to do it all right away. For instance, we feel we could paint the whole thangka tomorrow, make an exact replica of it. But this is not an art course on how to paint pictures; we are training you how to see things as they are.

When you see a thangka, you could just look—not in terms of it being a fantastic work of art, but as a simple visual object. Just look at it. Feel the difference between seeing a thangka and seeing someone have a car crash. See the stillness and the movement. This is not regarded as a fantastic contrast of metaphysical worlds, but as a simple visual perception. You can actually do it, you can see it. If you look too long, you will get bored, because you would like to see the next goodie; at this point it would be better to go very slowly. [See illustration facing page 48.]

Usually, we are restless with our visual perception. Even when we see something fantastically beautiful, we are shy in actually relating with it. That shyness is connected with aggression. We are unable to see things properly, as they really are. If we see beautiful things, we are so fascinated and interested: we would like to touch and handle them; we would like to smell them and hear them. On the other hand, when we see something ugly or terrible, such as dogshit on the street, we don't want to touch it, we don't want to see it, and we try to avoid the whole thing—"Yuck!"

It is very interesting how our mind and our psychology work, how perception conducts our life. But we really don't give in to it, we don't let go completely. That doesn't mean we have to eat dogshit or abandon beautiful things, but it's interesting how we reject things that have the slightest offensiveness to us. We don't like it at all. And if we do like something, if there's a slight suggestion of promise, we like it so much that we want to get right into it. The result is that usually we don't really *look* at anything at all. Particularly if we have lots of money, if we see a beautiful fabric, beautiful painting, or any beautiful item, we just want to buy it. That's our first impulse. Then we become afraid of it. We wonder whether it's worth buying, how much it costs, whether it's the real thing or not. We get panicky, step back a little, and get completely confused. By then, we have no idea whether we want it or not, our minds are so confused.

The problem comes from not being able to spend enough time looking at things as they are, directly, properly, clearly. That seems to be one of the basic points in how to view symbolism. It is a question of reality, how we view reality. You have an idea that when you begin to experience reality you are going to be entertained, that you won't have any more pain. But quite possibly seeing reality may be more painful. Ultimate reality may be more painful than any pain you experience in your life. That seems to be an important point. Although you would like to see things changing—not working out as they were, but reshuffling themselves—at the same time, the world remains as it is.

The Process of Perception

There is a kind of standing-still quality, or stalemate, in which comments and remarks become unimportant, and seeing things as they are becomes the real thing. It's like a frog sitting in the middle of a big puddle, with rain constantly falling on it. The frog simply winks its eyes at each raindrop that falls on it, but it doesn't change its posture.

The question of reality is a very confusing one. Nobody knows, but everybody knows that somebody knows. That seems to be the problem we are facing: maybe nobody knows at all or maybe everybody knows. So we should not purely trust the information, suggestions, and ideas that come to us from external sources, but actually work with ourselves and try to develop our own personal understanding and appreciation of reality. Reality seems to be the basic space in which we operate in our ordinary, everyday life. It brings some sense of comfort and, at the same time, some sense of confusion. There seems to be a basic play between the two.

When we begin to perceive our phenomenal world, we do not perceive it as purely gray and nondescript, as though it were camouflaged. In fact, we see highlights of all kinds. For example, when we perceive an ordinary object—when we take a look at an egg or a cup of tea—there's a sense of boredom, because such a thing is so ordinary and domestic. We already know what an egg is like, and we know what a cup of tea is like. But when we are presented with something extraordinary, we begin to feel we are being treated to a special show. So in either the ordinary or the excited state of mind, whether we find the world extremely boring or extraordinarily entertaining, there's always a sense of confusion and aggression.

Such aggression is an obstacle to visual dharma, to hearing and the other sense perceptions, and to understanding reality in its fullest sense. So some kind of fundamental discipline seems to be absolutely important and necessary. Without any actual practice of sitting meditation to enable us to make friends with ourselves, nothing can be heard or seen to its fullest extent; nothing can be perceived as we would like to perceive it. But slowly and naturally, through our discipline, we gradually begin to branch out into the real world, the world of chaos, pain, and anxiety.

When we reach the state of nonaggression, it is not that we cease to perceive anything, but we begin to perceive in a particular way. With the absence of aggression, there is further clarity, because nothing is based on anxiety and nothing is based on ideas or ideals of any kind. Instead, we are beginning to see things without making any demands. We are no longer trying to buy or sell anything to anybody. It is a direct and very personal experience.

Our experience of the state of nonaggression becomes so personal that sometimes it is quite painful. Because all obstacles of any kind have been completely cleared out, for the first time we are seeing things from the point of view of pure vision and clarity. We begin to hear music purely and see colors and visual objects in their fullest purity. When we become more sensitive to experiences in this way, they become more penetrating, and they begin to make more sense. Therefore, there is the possibility of irritation. But at the same time, there is also a lot of humor. We no longer feel that we have to hassle, or try to swim across this ocean of tremendous demands the world makes on us. We don't have to push against it anymore. There's a sense of clarity, which is extraordinarily pleasing, and at the same time, there is a sense of overwhelming precision, which makes our experience terribly painful. So we could say that this particular journey of seeing things as they are, experiencing the iconography and sacred art of the world, is a state of mind—as much as Bombay Gin.

In many cases, we try so hard to understand. We are so eager that our eagerness begins to become numbness. We are so eager that we misunderstand things a lot. Sometimes our mind becomes completely blank, and we can't actually communicate. We forget how to put our sentences together; we forget what to write down; we lose our memories. All kinds of problematic things take place in us as an expression of eagerness, which is a somewhat euphemistic term for mental speediness. But this is a long project. It is important to study and work with this material and to examine our life and our experience. We could learn to experience our world properly, so that our life becomes worth living and further learning takes place. We can perceive the world with lots of space, or we can perceive the world with no space, but that is saying the same thing. The experience of no space at the same time happens to be space. So when we begin to overcrowd the whole thing, the crowdedness becomes space.

Visual perception becomes reality gradually. According to the traditional pattern, beginning to see something visually is a process that has many levels. First we see with our eyes, then we smell with our eyes, then we hear with our eyes, and then we begin to touch the object with our eyes. Each particular sensory perception has those same aspects taking place. For instance, at the auditory level, when we hear something, we see it first, then we hear it, then we smell it, then we touch it. So psychological shifts take place all the time. Perceiving is a gradual process.

Realistically, when we *see* something and experience it personally, our first connection is made abruptly, impulsively. As we perceive further, we can *smell* that visual object: its texture, its setup, and the vibrations it presents to us. Then we begin to *hear* that visual object. We can hear its texture as well as its breath, whether it breathes hard or soft. We can actually hear the heartbeat of that visual object. So we see its heartbeat and hear it at the same time. Finally, because we have gone through this whole process, we begin to take an immense interest in that visual object, and we try to *touch* it visually. We commit ourselves to that particular perception, and we actually begin to relate with whatever goes on in our world. We begin to touch our world, to feel the real texture of it, not just the sound or smell or first visual flash of the texture. In that way, we are able to establish ourselves in total communication.

That process takes place all the time, in whatever we do in our life and at whatever perceptual level we are relating with. Whether it is our hearing system, smelling system, seeing system, or tasting system; whether we are eating food, hearing music, seeing visual things, wearing different types of clothes, or taking a swim, those four categories—sight, smell, hearing, and touch—take place all the time. That is how we actually perceive things as they are. However, sometimes we jump back and forth instead of going through the regular, gradual process of seeing things as they are properly. First we touch some kind of edge, then we bounce back from that edge, and then we return to it again. We begin to have a dialogue with ourselves, to tell ourselves a story: "Maybe this is not right, maybe this is not true, maybe this is the ideal situation. Let's talk about it, let's think about it." We go on and on and on that way, bouncing back and forth all the time. That is the neurotic, or psychotic, tendency in visual perception.

Visual perception does not have anything to do with whether or not we are seeing colors properly. Even if we are color-blind, we can still do it. When we begin to see something, first we have the question of visual perspective: the world we see is framed by our eyes, so it has a sort of oval shape, or egg shape. We can't see beyond the limitations of our eyes. Then we begin to smell, which goes on in the back of our head. We smell *behind* what we see. Some kind of commentator comes along and says that this object has a smell or odor to it. Not only that, but then we begin to hear that particular object from all around—not behind and in front alone, but underneath us and above us as well. We begin to sense that something is there, and we try to figure out what it might be. And finally, we begin to establish some kind of relationship. We begin to touch, which is a very direct and forward situation. We begin to feel it personally, and we try to make decisions, saying, "I'll buy it. I like it," or "I reject it. I don't like it." The whole process takes place in a fraction of a second, very fast. Jing! Jing! Jing! Jing! That whole mechanism is very fast and very simple, and it takes place all the time.

As far as dharma art or absolute experience is concerned, along with our experience we begin to see things as they are, touch on things as they are. Then we begin just to *be* with object perceptions, without accepting or rejecting. We simply try to *be* that way. There is a kind of standing-still quality, or stalemate, in which comments and remarks become unimportant, and seeing things as they are becomes the real thing. It's like a frog sitting in the middle of a big puddle, with rain constantly falling on it. The frog simply winks its eyes at each raindrop that falls on it, but it doesn't change its posture. It doesn't try either to jump into the puddle or to get out of the puddle. That quality is what is symbolized by a sitting bull, so the frog becomes a sitting bull.

Being and Projecting

In this practice, you go slowly through the threefold process of perception: the sense of being, the sense of doing, and the sense of linking together.

In the Buddhist tradition, it is said that there are six psychological sense perceptions—seeing, hearing, tasting, smelling, touching, and thinking—which operate on six corresponding types of sense objects. These are referred to as the twelve *ayatanas*. And according to Buddhist psychology, we go through a threefold process in connection with each of those sense perceptions. The first is a sense of existence. When you begin to listen or to look at something, you have a sense of being. This is just a general sense of being; nothing in particular is planned or conceptualized—simply a sense of being. Second, there is a flicker or snapping process, which flashes to the sense object. And third, there is communication between the two. Your flashing process and your sense of existence are brought together.

As a space awareness practice, we could work with our sense perceptions in that way, in a kind of slow-motion version of that. First you work with the sense of existence. You are standing and you are there. Feel that basic sense of being. Then, in order to prove that existence, you have to do something, to project out. Finally, you begin to feel some sort of play back and forth, as the projector and the projection relate together. So in this practice, you go slowly through the threefold process of perception: the sense of being, the sense of doing, and the sense of linking together.

In this exercise, we are trying to use some of the notions of Buddhist psychology in a practice. The whole process starts with an embryonic sense perception. Before you have actually seen the object or moved your body, there is the *potential* of using the sense organs. Then we use speech, hearing our own speech; visual perception; the movement of our body; and possibly we could smell the whole thing as well. The way in which we usually project ourselves is made into a sort of formula: you start with a sense of being, putting yourself into a situation, slowly dissolving the edge, and then executing whatever is there.

Obviously, the sense of being can't be one solid thing. It moves constantly. It projects out and in, and it is very fickle. Nevertheless, there should be some attempt to relate to the overall situation, to a sense of the whole. It is like looking at a string of beads or an animal's tail. When a lot of little beads are strung together, you have a *mala*; hundreds of small hairs put together become a tail. So there is a general sense of being, made out of lots of little things put together.

Lost Horizons

One day passes and another day comes along, and everything happens the same.
But basically, we are so afraid of the brilliance coming at us, and the sharp
experience of our life, that we can't even focus our eyes.

Relative symbolism is based on experiencing one's world in a different fashion.
This does not refer to some super spiritual materialistic vision based on altered
neurological perceptions. It simply means an experience that transcends the
common phenomena of good and bad, promises and threats. This kind of
visual perception is fundamental and basic, and it can only develop through
training in the discipline of meditation. Without such training, without such
taming of the mind, we either misjudge situations or are overpowered by
them. We are unable to perceive things as they are in the fullest sense.

People struggle in all kinds of ways to realize and understand a higher level
of vision. Sometimes we catch a glimpse of it in the work of great artists, such
as William Blake or Shakespeare. We constantly try to reach higher and
higher, as if we were dwarves. But we do not need to regard ourselves as
dwarves. It is always possible for us to pick up on certain highlights and
principles of absolute visual dharma. At first they may not be continuous
experiences but occur to us in a haphazard and accidental way. So we might
have a problem with that, as it is not quite in keeping with our speed and our
desire to learn more.

There is also a lot of room. Because of that, when you actually do begin
to perceive things in your own true way, you find that the perceptions you are
experiencing can be extremely painful and irritating. It hurts a lot, like looking at the sun with our naked eyes. It is overly powerful. *The Tibetan Book of
the Dead* talks about how we shy away from brilliant and penetrating visions,
but when we see something subdued and pleasant, we are magnetized. It is
quite possible we might go along with those inviting visions rather than the

penetrating ones. But *The Tibetan Book of the Dead* also says that if you go along with the bright and penetrating visions, you might be saved; whereas if you are fascinated by the beautiful, fantastic, colorful visions, you might be trapped in the samsaric rebirth cycle again and again.

We have problems with the kind of visual perceptions that dominate our life. People are generally afraid to jump into a high-energy pool; they prefer to latch on to a moderate, toned-down, monotone energy. That seems to be much simpler and cheaper. What's wrong with us, if I may say so, is that we are too cowardly. We might think we are extremely brave and able, that we can fight anyone who fights us, overcome them with logical debates and put our points across clearly. We might think we are completely well equipped, with all the defense mechanisms we need—and not only that, but all the offensive weapons as well. People do feel that way sometimes, but even that is an act of cowardice. We are so paranoid that we want to be prepared for any possible danger. We want to shield ourselves from the reality of fear. We would like to see something very gentle and colorful. But if we look very closely at our desire for something gentle and colorful, as opposed to the brightness, we find that basically we just want to get sick. We prefer to be nauseated rather than to be excited by the pool of energy. If we are sick, it is easy to say, "I'm sorry, but I have an upset stomach. I must lie down. Please forgive me. I can't take part in your party." We are so convincing. We are constantly looking for a way to chicken out.

We really don't want to deal with the bright lights, the very precise, sharp, penetrating, cutting brilliance. Nobody would like to work with that; instead, there is hesitation. People often resort to devotion as a way of chickening out: "If I trust and worship what I have experienced, probably the brilliant radiation will not hurt me, but accept me." Another possibility is to philosophize the whole thing: "Since my philosophical understanding is quite a friendly one, I might be saved and accepted in my vision of sharp, penetrating experience." We could quite safely say that both of those are attempts to shield ourselves, because we are afraid of the bright, precise, penetrating realities of life. We don't want to have anything to do with it, if possible.

Sometimes you feel embarrassed that you are put on the spot. You feel you must make some attempt to deal with it, or at least pay lip service to it, saying, "That's a fantastic experience, so penetrating, so powerful. Okay, I'm going to do it!" Or we make a big deal out of it, "Here I am, naked! I'm just about to jump off the cliff! Pain or pleasure, I don't care—here I come!" But when we are actually put on the spot, we can't do it. Whether we are subtle or dramatic, it's still just lip service. All of us without exception are cowards. We know the consequences, but we are not willing to leap. The penetrating experiences in our life are extremely powerful, unshakable, so true. That does not only apply to visual perception, but also to emotional experience: visual perception and emotional experience always go together.

Visual perception is the first gate, or entrance, through which we relate with our emotions. And when the object of our emotions is not literally visible, in front of our eyes, we psychologically imagine the visual perception, and we begin to feel the emotion. For example, when we love someone very dearly, painfully so, we frequently have visual perceptions of that person. That builds up to creating imaginary conversations. He speaks to you, you speak to him. You develop a feeling of physical contact, maybe eating in a restaurant together or driving around in the country. All those perceptions are connected to visual perception. Visual perception is the vanguard of all the other sense perceptions. The second level is auditory experience.

We are extraordinarily fertile and have immense potential, but at the same time, we don't really want to commit ourselves. We prefer to lie back and nest in our neurosis and rest and rest, like an ingrown toenail. Sometimes we get bored and try to entertain ourselves. But we are so polite and childish, whether we go to the movies, eat in fine restaurants, have a few drinks with friends, or take a trip to Asia or Europe if we have money. We do all kinds of little things, but they are not *real* things. What we are doing is not quite what we should be doing. You might regard yourself as a blunt and direct person, but you're still being too polite. You might vomit your neurosis right and left—shout and yell at people, fight and kill, make love—but you are still back to square one. We are such cowards. It's so embarrassing that we can't talk about it or even think about it. What's the point of all these little secrets, these little games that we play? We seem to enjoy them. One day passes and another day comes along, and everything happens the same. But basically, we are so afraid of the brilliance coming at us, and the sharp experience of our life, that we can't even focus our eyes.

We are afraid, and we don't really want to relate with anything at all. We feel somewhat awkward. Sometimes we deal with our awkwardness very professionally, as in talking to the policeman who stops us on the highway. And sometimes we deal with it by acting like we were talking to our kids. But none of those little tactics work. Those imitation professional tactics don't click. At that point, we don't see anything, we don't hear anything, we don't speak. We are blind, deaf, and mute. This is the basic process we go through, and we should do something about it. It is very important to do something, because we are not completely paralyzed yet. There is still a lot of energy. We can actually begin to face reality as it is. I don't see any problem with that.

The problem boils down to the fact that we do not really want to experience reality in the fullest sense at all. Instead, we always try to bring in a substitute reality. For instance, if we find that our child is not going along with our expectations, we say, "One day this child will come to his senses and come back to us." If we have a lost lover, we say, "Sooner or later he will return to me and realize how I really feel about him." Even with a lost pet, a lost dog or cat, we hope that it will return and recognize us. Those little gestures are somewhat pathetic and don't make much sense. With LSD or any kind of drug experience, when the first trip is terrible, we would like to make the second trip better, so we take it again. "I was just on the verge of discovering something when I was on my fifth trip. Maybe I should take a sixth." That approach perpetuates itself all the time, but it never catches the fish in the net. And in the world of art, we could take the same superficial approach, in which everything is very interesting and very beautiful and then the whole thing is over. The memory of what you have gone through does not even take part in your dreams. Everything is forgotten, a lost horizon.

Giving

Aggression acts like a big veil preventing us from seeing the precision of the functioning of absolute symbolism, as well as relative symbolism. And the only possible remedy, according to the traditional approach, is surrendering.

Approaching symbolism based on our desire constantly to learn more and more is questionable, because a lot of aggression is taking place there. Not in the sense of being angry, or losing your temper, but aggression as a fundamental obstacle. All the collections you have made, and continue to make, are questionable. When you get really angry, your eyes are bloodshot and you can't see properly; you begin to stutter and you can't speak properly. You become a mean vegetable. That kind of aggression is the greatest obstacle to perception and to perceiving symbolism. If you really see the city of Boulder, if you really see the mountains of Boulder or the skies of Boulder, there is no aggression. But I somewhat doubt that you have really seen it. This remark is not condescending, putting down your honorable existence. It is a reminder. Maybe you haven't got anything together to experience what you should experience. That's highly possible, because aggression is very powerful. When you project toward an object, you want to capture it, as a spider captures a fly, and suck its blood. You may feel refreshed, but that is a big problem. The definition of dharma art, as well as iconography, is the personal experience of nonaggression.

There is more to aggression than losing your temper and beating your husband or your wife or your kid or having a fight with your neighbors. All of that is simply a by-product of aggression. Actual aggression takes place in our minds, in our hearts. It makes our blood boil. It can make us so completely stupid and offended that we cannot even see. At that point, very strangely, you reach a kind of pseudo-experience of egolessness. You become completely one with the aggression. When you really lose your temper, you

don't exist; only your aggression exists. You lose your reference point. That is
what you are most afraid of. You are so outraged, you see red, your heart beats
very fast, and you begin to hear this low-pitched sound. And you end up just
a little bundle of a flea, red in color, a flea who would like to jump but can't,
a mean, bloodthirsty flea. You may think you're big, but you're just a flea.

Aggression creates a lot of obstacles to experiencing symbolism. When
we talk about aggression, people get angry. They don't want to hear any of
it; they want nothing to do with it. "Tell me something peaceful, good.
You're supposed to calm my mind." I'm afraid the truth of the matter is it
doesn't work that way. We have to explore what we have, and how deafness
and blindness come about because of our personal aggression. When we are
aggressive, we would like to find something out very badly. We would like
to possess the truth, chew it, swallow it, and eat it up. That is a big problem.
We demand truth as we would a piece of chocolate. But we are still angry and
always want more. So we look for the next block of chocolate. We go on like
that and never realize how many trips we lay on ourselves. That makes us
deaf, dumb, and blind. Our perception of symbolism is completely blocked.
That is a very terrifying, terrifying space.

Aggression acts like a big veil preventing us from seeing the precision of
the functioning of absolute symbolism, as well as relative symbolism. And
the only possible remedy, according to the traditional approach, is surrendering. That seems to be the only way to overcome aggression. Surrendering does
not mean reducing yourself to a child jumping into someone's lap, looking
for parents. Surrendering is simply wanting to give, to let go of all kinds of
personal trips, economic trips, and spiritual trips involved in holding back.
Holding back, or aggression, only makes us more blind. So giving up, opening, surrendering, is very important, because you finally begin to let go of
your aggression. You begin to say, "Get the hell out!"

You feel you would like to give, to open, to take a leap. Depending on
the level of your understanding, that might even mean giving in to your own
aggression, letting that aggression take you over. You couldn't care less. You
have some faith and trust in the basic truth coming from the lineage that
actually speaks the truth of nonaggression. It is such a relief when you begin
to give and give and give. I don't mean the conventional idea of giving, where

if you have ten dollars in your bank account, you might give five and keep the other five for your upkeep. Giving away fifty percent of your aggression and reserving the other fifty percent for holding your trip together is not quite enough. You have to give up the whole thing. And each time you give, your vision begins to clear, and there's less of a filter over your pupils; your hearing begins to clear, and there's less wax on your eardrums. So you begin to hear and see much better as you give up more and more of this uptightness, this holding back, this resentment. You're not doing anybody a favor particularly, and there is no one to say thank you, like a country parson thanking you for giving money to the church, which may seem fake. You don't give it to anybody; you just give it away without expecting anything in return. You just give, give, give, let go. Each time you give, more clarity takes place, and you are better able to see the real meaning of symbolism. The twofold reality of relative and absolute symbolism can be seen very clearly.

Giving and opening oneself is not particularly painful, when you begin to do it. But the idea of giving and opening is very painful. When you are asked to give, to take a leap, it feels terrible. You don't want to do it, although you are somewhat tickled by the idea. "Maybe I'll make some kind of breakthrough or maybe I'll lose everything." Let's go along with that inquisitive mind and give, open further, open completely! Sooner or later we're going to do it, so the sooner the better. I hope this is not too complicated. Basically the only thing we are discussing is giving. It is quite simple: giving and the absence of aggression.

Once you give, once you open your eyes and ears and everything is completely cleaned up, when everything has been seen through completely, the end result is a sudden experience of precision. It is so precise and clear that it is like getting new spectacles or a new hearing aid. The whole thing becomes so precise and so direct that it's painful. You want to go back to your old fucked-up system: "I'd rather be deaf than hear this. I'd rather be blind than see that." In some sense, that is like what the entire older generation is saying, because they don't want to see their children growing up in their own way. That is a problem for a lot of parents. So we end up in a very complicated situation. We are seeing so much that we can't handle it—things are so precise, so direct, and so true. "How can we protect ourselves from the truth?

Let's run back and reject the whole thing, let's lie a little bit. Let's cover our heads with blankets and pretend nothing has happened and go back to the past, the fantastic, dirty, neurotic, juicy, good old days. We prefer that." It is very possible that we would like to go back and degrade ourselves. If we are forced to see too much, we would like to reduce ourselves to infants, go back to our mother's womb and become an embryo, or maybe a sperm, and then just disappear altogether. But we can do better than that.

Let's face the facts of reality and its precision, which is so irritating and powerful. Once we begin to experience its workings and the texture, once we really perceive it, it is no longer problematic. The reason it could become problematic is because we are not inquisitive enough to perceive the symbolism or signs that come up or occur to us. But we now can experience the symbolism precisely and directly. Having taken the leap, having abandoned home ground, you are like a naked child without preconceptions. You can experience the symbolism on the spot. You can do that. You are clear, precise, and direct. And that precision becomes very powerful and important.

Let's not complain about the past; it is such a waste of energy. You could do a lot of things for humankind if you could come out and be precise. Let us face the world without wearing sunglasses. Take off your glasses and perceive the light. That is very much needed. You can do so much, not only for yourself but for others. You could contribute so much help and service to people who are suffering, who are trapped in all kinds of problems. You are not dead yet, and you can't pretend to be dead. Sometimes you might feel you would like to join the dead world so nobody would bother you, but it's not as simple as that. There is life after death. Things are not as simple as you think. You can't just act on impulse. You have to give more.

So please pay some consideration to this mutual world of ours. We create this world mutually. Maybe it's not so good, not so beautiful, but it's not so bad either—it's a regular world. You can get along in this world, and once you begin to relate with the world, you can appreciate the idea of symbolism. Aggression and paranoia, being unable to leap, are obstacles to symbolism. But once we stop rejecting the world, the world begins to pounce on us. Symbolism is imposed on us. Realizations and perceptions of all kinds of realities begin to take shape. There is symbolism right and left and front and back.

Self-Existing Humor

*The separation between "you" and "I," you and your world, you and your God,
is cut through by a sense of humor.*

It is very important to appreciate your world: the place you live, your lifestyle,
your style of cooking, your style of viewing the visual world altogether. Basically, you've got to know who you are and what you are, to begin with;
otherwise, you will just be another agent selling the dharma for your own
benefit. If you appreciate your world, then you might pick something up that
personally benefits your spiritual journey and increases your wisdom. You
could see the world as it is, with its own perspective, and with a touch of
insight. You could learn how to look at a needle on a pine tree, how to smell
a raccoon, how to drink a cup of tea, how to feel your hair, your dress, your
clothes, how to touch your feet on the ground, how to walk. At the perceptual
level, everything is artistic in some sense, but there has to be communication
and real perception. Without that we have a big barrier. I don't feel like
talking to anybody, if they have no actual interest in life. If you're only interested in recapturing information about thangkas, you would be better off
studying Mexican cooking or learning how to make horseshoes. Symbolism is
not simply an art-school project—it's much more serious than that. There is
a lot of power behind the whole thing.

  Certain energies take place in you when you begin to view visual dharma.
Having understood symbolism in general and your perceptual world—the
world of phenomena that is colorful, nasty, exciting, helpful, and all the
rest—something actually takes place in your visual perception. You can't
avoid it. We are trying to take that particular essence and work with it. The
essence of that perception is not a work of art but a lifestyle that can be shared
throughout your life. Walking on the sidewalk, crossing at the red light,

watching your eggs in the frying pan, listening to the tea kettle whistling—the little things in life are the most important.

Ultimately, there are three levels to viewing symbolism or visual dharma. These levels apply to dharma painting as well as the dharma pictures that exist spontaneously in your life. First you need a *sense of humor,* which is based on an understanding as to how things work. Ordinarily, people have the idea that humor means you must be laughing at somebody behind their back, or that you think everything is corny and funny and doesn't make any sense. There is immense aggression in that; such humor is crude and resentful. But in this case, humor is some kind of delight. We begin to learn something about how reality works, not by studying scholastically but by perceiving how humor exists within the cosmic world. With that kind of humor, we begin to see through the separateness of me and others, others and me. The separation between "you" and "I," you and your world, you and your God, is cut through by a sense of humor. That is the basic point.

After that we come up with the second level: *basic space,* in which humor is self-existent. We begin to see the manifestation of a cosmic structure. It is very personal, very ordinary, and very matter-of-fact—nothing divine or blissed out, particularly. There is some kind of complete, open space, ground that has never been messed up by plowing or by sowing seeds—complete virgin territory.

At the third level, experience becomes much more realistic, much more grounded and personal. The perceiver, or person with a sense of humor, is beginning to be able to relate with things as they are very closely and precisely. That *precision* has all kinds of sharp edges. The idea of peace, the idea of harmony, the idea of aggression or negativity—all things are included. So visual dharma is based on having these three foundations: a nonindividualistic sense of humor, a sense of all-pervasive space, and an appreciation of the play of phenomena.

At the beginning, there is a person with a sense of humor. Then there is a perception—which is a big, wide-open, empty sky, bright blue in color. Finally, there is a little comet coming out of the blue sky—or maybe a little cloud, or maybe a little bird begins to fly, or a bigger bird, or an airplane. Something takes place in your openness that begins to change the mood. The openness is acknowledged by the different tones of energy that take place. Peaceful energy is benevolent, pacifying, harmless. There is a sense of warmth and encouragement. Wrathful energy is mocking, exposing. Our caricature is exposed and starts to churn up. Sometimes it's savage and deadly; sometimes it's dignified and powerful. That all takes place quite simply.

Then, having already developed those experiences, we have some sense of understanding the teachings of enlightenment. We begin to appreciate reality in its fullest sense. All the experiences we are going through are somewhat workable. And it is not just your lonely trip, but somebody has done it already. Somebody has the idea and the information and the lineage behind it. So there is a sense of the warmth of the guru, helper, spiritual friend, elder, master, medicine man, or whatever you'd like to call it. Finally, you come down to earth, where those experiences are not all that outrageous or fantastic, but *real.*

Outrageousness

I don't think you learn dharma art, you discover it; and you do not teach dharma art, but you set up an environment so it can be discovered.

Dharma art is based on energy and conviction. In this regard, the perceptions of everyday life are seen as a resource, or working basis, for both the work of art and the practice of meditation. But there seems to be a need for two further types of energy—the energy of nonaggression and the energy of outrageousness.

Generally, outrageousness is a product of extending oneself: you can't contain yourself, therefore you become outrageous. You tend to spill over what you can't contain in your container. But that doesn't seem to be the case here. Outrageousness here is a sense of direct conviction, in which you feel intense humor, or intense energy and power, penetrating inside. Such outrageousness seems to be necessary, but it has to be accompanied by nonaggression. The question of nonaggression is based on whether you perceive your particular world in connection with glorifying your existence and your ego in the neurotic sense, or whether it is free from that.

That's very definite. But there seem to be mixed feelings in people's minds—inspiration is mixed with ego-centeredness. Somehow, that mixture tends to produce a sense of blindness in which you are unable to see the panoramic vision of a given situation, and consequently you are unable to act accordingly. So there's a problem with being self-centered, if there is aggression as well as self-consciousness. Self-consciousness alone doesn't seem to be a particularly big problem. In fact, sometimes there's room for being self-conscious: the constant checking, constant reviewing, might be a source of further cynicism toward one's ego, which could be desirable. But definitely aggression is a big problem.

Aggression is based on wanting to demonstrate something that you

know, wanting to tell somebody the truth you have discovered. Although your demonstration might be okay, even fantastic, and the truth you have discovered may be relevant, the means and way the whole thing is presented seems to be a problem. From that point of view, we can't have rules and regulations as to what to say and what not to say, how to act and how not to act, particularly. The whole thing has to be genuinely intuitive. The medium, or the style that we use in presenting the truth, seems to be the crux of the matter. In other words, an artist may be able to present his or her work of art precisely and thoroughly. But a work of art doesn't come out purely transparent, without personality. A work of art always has the smell, so to speak, or the feelings of whoever produced that particular work of art. For instance, the smell and feeling of that person could be extraordinarily aggressive. In that case, no matter what the actual representations may be, the person behind it has a lot of aggression, so more garbage is involved. The question of nonaggression is extremely important. Nonaggression makes art the art of dharma, or truth—real art. Such art has a sense of real simplicity, without any handles attached. We only want to exhibit our work of art, perform our work of art, or live with our work of art.

In a lot of art there is a tendency to try to capture a glimpse of one moment of experience and make it into a solid eternity. We have some brilliant idea and we try to make it into a piece of art. But that is captured art. We try to capture our artistic talent in a particular work of art—a piece of music, a painting, a poem. Until that work of art is forgotten or destroyed, it is stuck on a piece of paper or on a canvas or on a record that can be listened to over and over. It seems that such an attempt to solidify one's work of art, instead of giving birth to artistic talent, creates death for artistic talent.

We could shift our allegiance from death to life. In that case, art becomes a living continuity and is seen as a perpetual process. First somebody has an idea. The idea is presented in a very embryonic stage at the beginning. It begins as a seed, but then that embryonic essence begins to sprout and to make shoots. As it continues to develop and grow, it makes little flower buds. That concept of art is based on the idea of living. The basic point is that there is a sense of continuity in your understanding of life.

If you know who you are, what you are, where you are, and you have something to say about that, you could share it with your fellow human beings. That's fine. There's nothing wrong with that, as long as you don't want to publicize it. And even if you do want to publicize your embryonic discoveries, you don't spell out the whole thing at once. It is very tempting to spell everything out, which proves one's legitimacy, one's wisdom, or one's artistry. But according to the Buddhist tradition, in communicating with the world, particularly in the realm of art, the only thing you can do is hint, just give a basic headline. It depends on your attitude. If you want to demonstrate something very badly and you achieve that, then your work of art is a dead one. But if you present your work of art as a completely full message *without* spelling out every word of it, then you have just given the public a corner of what you might say. Therefore it is still fertile in people's minds and there is room for it to unfold. It is living art.

If you expound more than is necessary, it becomes apologetic. And it is boring because the audience begins to follow the logic while you are still standing on it. And you begin to pounce on it at the same time. I think the problem is that people are afraid they might be ignored, they might become failures, so they end up explaining everything they know, all the reference points at once. That attitude of poverty or failure makes your theater dirt, your poetry dirt. Usually the sense of something unsaid but implied makes more sense to people. It is not particularly holding back the truth, it is being honest and at the same time festive about what you have to say. Then art is a living process.

Nonaggression doesn't mean there is a regulation or cutting down of anything. Nonaggression is a product of awakened realization. You don't usually feel a sense of inhibition when you awake during the day from sleep. You just go about your everyday life, because awake and asleep are different. And of course you don't try to fall asleep in the middle of your activities during the day. But at the same time, you don't feel that you are inhibited from anything because you are not sleeping. Nonaggression is an organic process rather than a discipline or moral binding. Nonaggression is seeing through the aggression and realizing there are more ways to be active and efficient than being aggressive; it is realizing a new angle of energy.

In the case of meditation practice, either we do it at the simple, matter-

71

of-fact level or we do it with a very meaningful religious or philosophical undertone. That undertone automatically becomes dogma and belief, and that belief becomes a very definite belief. Because that belief is very definite, therefore you should defend that belief. And defending that belief becomes aggression. The quality of outrageousness is the opposite of that—or the extension of that act without aggression. The definition of outrageousness is basically a sense of humor. In this case, humor is not particularly making fun and mocking somebody or something. Instead, it is an appreciative gesture. That is, things don't seem to be as heavy as we think they are, but they seem to be floating above the ground, and seemingly hilarious, funny, swift, and lucid.

At the same time, humor is not particularly casual or haphazard. The casual approach to life is often the result of being shy and feeling self-conscious and tense, so you would like to pass the buck or divert the attention to some other situation. But that also diverts the concentration of attitude and energy, so it is basically stupid rather than insightful. Humor is not like buying toys for your kids, which is somewhat lighthearted—unless the toy turns out to be extraordinarily expensive. And it is not at the level of the cheap world of plastics or teddy bears. It comes from delight and a sense of celebration. A sense of humor from that point of view is very transparent; at the same time, it is very definite. It has its own background and sanity.

Outrageousness is a question of being fearless in your celebration and your sense of humor. Sometimes it could be somewhat absurd and stubborn, but that seems to be the necessary eccentricity of this particular approach. Again, as long as it doesn't contain aggression and an exhibitionistic outlook, it seems to be quite simple. A sense of conviction brings fearlessness, outrageousness, and a sense of humor. And that basic sense of groundlessness and nonexistence brings up the question of aggression in the practice of art.

In dealing with aggression, we can't really separate ourselves into professional artists, amateur artists, and meditators. At the same time, somebody could be both a professional and an amateur artist and a meditator as well. Those areas are all related. Dharma art does not involve tricks or have to do with training artists in the Buddhist scheme. But our attitude toward art has to be expanded. This society in particular thrives on pigeonholing everybody's style and discipline into categories, which becomes very clumsy and imprisoning.

You could try to continue your artwork and your meditation together, whatever you do in your life and whatever job you might have. I don't think you learn dharma art, you discover it; and you do not teach dharma art, but you set up an environment so it can be discovered. It's like preparing a nice meditation hall, with nice cushions to sit on, so it's inviting for you to sit and take part in meditation practice. The makers of the meditation hall and the cushions can't make you meditate, particularly—that's what you can do. And that is dharma art, it seems to me.

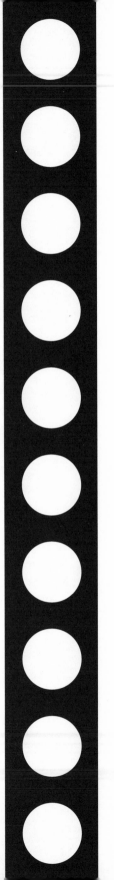

Wise Fool

We have to allow ourselves to realize that we are complete fools; otherwise, we have nowhere to begin. We have to be willing to be a fool and not always try to be a wise guy. We could almost say that being willing to be a fool is one of the first wisdoms.

In order to experience some perspective on reality, we need to have a clear understanding, free from motivation, and also a sense of delight, or humor. Such an understanding of our perceptions only comes from a sense of nonterritoriality—that is to say, giving up ego's clinging, aggression, grasping, and all the rest of it. So there is a need for immense openness without frivolity, immense inquisitiveness without aggression.

Before we can perceive and understand the subtleties of visual dharma, or any subtleties that exist in our life in general, we must prepare ourselves properly. If we are not properly prepared, it will be quite dangerous to play games with the energies of life. The danger comes from doing things wrong, or possibly from doing things seemingly right, but at the wrong time. If we are not actually trying to make a connection with reality—properly, generously, and gently—then every move we might make in our life is wrong. Whether we are trying to move to a new apartment, another city, another state; trying to take up a new career or job; trying to develop a new interest in this or that—all those moves we might make seem to be successive disasters. Everything goes wrong, one thing after another, all the time. Something wrong is happening, but who should we blame? We could say, "I'm under some kind of spell, black magic. I made an enemy of somebody somewhere a long time ago, and that person is trying to throw a curse on me. That's why things are going wrong." But that's not quite true. We would always like to have a scapegoat to blame for the phenomenal world, but by doing so, we only make ourselves more blind, more deaf, and more mute.

The phenomenal world is purely self-existing in nature; it does not take either praise or blame. It is self-existing, but if we fail to relate with the phenomenal world properly, something happens. Some kind of message comes to us which is not particularly organized by the people upstairs, but rather by the ground-floor people, ourselves. In other words, whatever direction we might take, we always need visual dharma. If we don't have true perception of visual dharma, a lot of things can go wrong.

On the one hand, there's the chicken-or-the-egg-first question. "In order to perceive visual dharma, don't we have to have an ideal situation first? Shouldn't something be done about that as well?" Seemingly there's no end to doing things wrong, messing things up all the time. And since we don't have a good starting point, nothing can go right. We are sort of trapped in that kind of negative "oy vey" situation. On the other hand, very interestingly, there is lots of room to make mistakes. That's true, absolutely true. But such room for mistakes cannot be created unless there is surrendering, giving, some kind of opening. It cannot take place if there's no basis for it. However, if there is some basis—if we can give away our aggression or attempt to give it away, if we attempt to open up and to strip away our territoriality and possessiveness—then there is lots of room for making mistakes. That doesn't necessarily mean there is room for dramatic mistakes, but lots of little dribbles of mistakes can take place, which usually occur in any case—we can't avoid it.

We have to allow ourselves to realize that we are complete fools; otherwise, we have nowhere to begin. We have to be willing to be a fool and not always try to be a wise guy. We could almost say that being willing to be a fool is one of the first wisdoms. So acknowledging foolishness is always a very important and powerful experience. The phenomenal world can be perceived and seen properly if we see it from the perspective of being a fool. There is very little distance between being a fool and being wise; they are extremely close. When we are really, truly fools, when we actually acknowledge our foolishness, then we are way ahead. We are not even in the process of becoming wise—we are already wise. Our journey generally takes place with that kind of shiftiness, in which everything overlaps. If we are taking the right direction in the present step, then we are not so afraid to get into the next step. And that means that we are actually well advanced on the next step already, maybe halfway through.

The perception of visual dharma plays an extremely important part in how we run our lives. It is not about becoming a famous art collector with a great understanding of Tibetan iconography, but it has to do with how we can "improve" our life, so to speak. Improving does not mean competitiveness, trying to get better so we can outsmart the other wise guys. Instead, it is taking some responsibility for our life. We are not just saying, "Wow! Isn't that a nice full moon. Isn't that a nice autumn tree. Fantastic!"—and thinking that is practicing visual dharma. Somehow, that doesn't quite do it. It is too adolescent, we could almost say cheap. A lot of dignity is required. Such dignity comes from taking immense interest in the details of our life and from having a sense of appreciation that a lot of experiences are coming into our lives. That allows us to be solid, down to earth, and basically right. The visual perception of iconography and symbolism can occur without watching a slide show, without flipping through books, taking trips to museums, or buying and selling thangkas. If the Buddhist teaching makes sense, it should make sense on every level. Otherwise, it's as you say, "bullshit," and everything goes down the drain. How do we go about it so that it makes sense? Actually, we don't go about it at all. Instead, we could just *be,* very simply, and watch ourselves.

The passion, aggression, and ignorance that go on in our mind are the first set of iconography ever presented in Buddhist doctrine. The Wheel of Life is just a simple chart of our ordinary, everyday life—our domestic world, emotional world, economic world, and political world. It shows how things work very basically. So before we realize or understand—or even become just about to understand—anything at all, we have to have some understanding of how things begin on the kitchen-sink level. We have to understand the ordinary, basic, very mundane, extremely mundane, and maybe too-secular level. We have to begin beyond so-called religion.

If we have an iconographic understanding of the redness of our desire, the blackness of our aggression, and the grayness of our ignorance, then at least we can begin to see some of the patterns in our life. We can begin to understand how all this visualization takes place in our life, in our world.

Those patterns are not just made-up patterns, but patterns that exist in our heads, in our minds, in our hearts. From that, slowly and definitely, some kind of journey takes place. We are discovering and rediscovering and re-rediscovering ourselves all the time.

We might say, "What's so good about rediscovering ourselves? We know ourselves already. We're full of shit, not so good. We know that anyway." But we don't. That's precisely the point. We think we are sick, but we have no idea how sick we are. That's a problem. If we knew how sick we were, we would be on the way to advising the doctor as to what kind of treatment we should receive. Then some kind of positive step could be taken quite fearlessly and basically. It could be a gentle step. We don't have to exhaust ourselves in a panic just because we are sick, or because these things happen every day as recurring situations, and life is quite a drag. We can take things step by step. We can reorganize our lives according to our situation, and do it slowly and precisely.

As we go on, little pimples begin to burst in our lives, little uptightnesses begin to resolve, little bubbles of emotionalism begin to burst themselves into nowhere out of the openness, and things begin to cook. At a given point, we may experience that we are cooking too much or not cooking enough. But those problems are always arbitrary: when we are in a good mood, we think we are doing well, that we are well cooked; but when we are not doing so well, we feel we are undercooked, and things are getting sterile and stagnant. It goes on and on. Pros and cons and pros and cons, one after another, take place all the time, but they are not particularly a big deal. The important point is to wake ourselves up each time we are cooked, so to speak.

Humor and inquisitive mind are happening constantly. Sometimes the world becomes very bright, extraordinarily bright. The brightness and the articulation of the world seem to become a hang-up, and we are almost tempted to close our eyes and ears. But having failed in that, we still go on. And sometimes it's more a nuisance: the world becomes more of a nuisance, and the path becomes more of a nuisance as well. The whole journey is just driving us crazy—such a nuisance, such a problem. That's where the need for bravery comes in. If we begin to be brave, we will be able to see how phenomena work. That is to say, we will really *see* how phenomena work, rather than having an intellectual or case-history kind of understanding of phenomena. We will see how phenomena work, how the world works, how things operate in our lives. At that point, experience becomes very penetrating. Some kinds of understanding or realization are hard to take, but we need to push further, to take an immense leap all the time. We need very much to take that kind of leap. Sometimes, looking back, we wonder why we are doing all this, and sometimes we think, why not? Sometimes there is no choice, and sometimes there is a choice, but we would like to find some contrast to that choice. So we have all kinds of relationships to the path, almost love affairs.

This particular journey is not a very easy one, absolutely not easy at all. It demands a lot from us. There's so much demand, but at the same time, some element of gentleness begins to arise in us. We might say we become carefree, but that does not necessarily mean being devoid of responsibility. We begin to realize that life is quite rich, apart from the complaints—and even the complaints seem to be quite colorful. We begin to pick up percolating bubbles here and there, which begin to crack up, and we begin to find that after all, maybe life is worth celebrating. Something is taking place; no complaints need to be made at this point. Everything is churning up and processing through all along. Something is definitely beginning to take place, which is pleasant—not particularly pleasurable, but pleasant. And why not? It makes sense, although that's not the point.

We actually feel it, we actually experience it. There's something very humorous and delightful about the whole thing. But once more, the clarity begins to become an irritating problem. More and more bright visions come to our heads, which doesn't mean we begin to see bunny rabbits or Jehovah riding on a cat. The bright vision I am talking about is the experience of redness, the experience of blueness, the experience of greenness, the experience of yellowness. It includes all the perceptual levels of phenomenal experience, rather than vision alone. Our life becomes worthwhile. We begin to appreciate something or other, although we still do not know exactly what. And somehow, even trying to find out whether we know anything about it doesn't seem to be a problem.

However, in the back of our minds, there may be some kind of problem: we may come along and actually want to find something out. And we may not find what we want, absolutely not. Our questions may not be answered one by one. But something else is taking place. Maybe the question mark itself is beginning to rot, become disheveled, and turn into a period, full stop. Maybe that is happening. It's a possibility. And that seems to be the process of the whole journey: dissolving the question mark into a full stop. The question mark becomes a statement or an exclamation, rather than a hollow line longing to be filled by answers.

Five Styles of Creative Expression

You could work with the five buddha family principles by picking up a piece of stone or a twig and approaching it from each of its five different aspects. With each family, a whole different perspective will begin to develop.

In discussing general aesthetic appreciation and creative work, I would like to discuss five styles, traditionally known as the five buddha families. By working with the five buddha families, we are trying to develop some basic understanding of how to see things in their absolute essence, their own innate nature. We can use this knowledge with regard to painting or poetry or arranging flowers or making films or composing music. It is also connected with relationships between people. The five buddha family principles seem to cover a whole new dimension of perception. They are very important at all levels of perception and in all creative situations.

In tantric iconography, the five buddha families are arrayed in the center and the four cardinal points of a mandala. The *buddha* family is in the center. It is the basic coordinate, basic wisdom, and is symbolized by a wheel and the color blue. *Vajra* is in the east and is connected with the dawn. It is symbolized by the color white and by the vajra scepter.* It is the sharpness of experience, as in the morning when we wake up. *Ratna* is in the south. It is associated with richness and is symbolized by a jewel and the color yellow. Ratna is connected with midday, when we begin to need refreshment and nourishment. *Padma* is in the west and is symbolized by the lotus and the color red. As our day grows older, we relate with recruiting a lover. It is time to socialize. Or, if we have fallen in love with an antique or with some clothing, it is time to go out and buy it. The last family is *karma,* in the north. It is symbolized by a sword and the color green. Finally we have captured the

*Editor's note: Sometimes the colors of these two families are reversed, in which case buddha is associated with white and vajra with blue.

whole situation: we have everything we need, and there is nothing more to get. So the mandala of the five buddha families represents the progress of a whole day or a whole course of action. We won't go through the philosophy; we'll start with the functions of these five principles and their association with composition. There are so many things to say about them, but basically vajra is white and water; ratna is yellow and earth; padma is red and fire; buddha is blue and space or sky; karma is green and wind.

Buddha is in the middle and, being in the middle, is the foundation or the basic ground. This basic ground is usually rather dull because it is too solid. We might have to dig it up and put concrete there, since it is rather uninteresting as it is. It will be interesting only if we know we are going to construct something on it.

Buddha is in the middle because it is the foundation rather than because it is the most important. Buddha could also be the environment, or the oxygen that makes it possible for the other principles to function. It has that sedate, solid quality. In terms of visuals, it is the uninteresting part, the waiting for something to happen. Often the buddha quality is necessary to create contrast between the other colorful types: vajra, ratna, padma, and karma. We need buddha as the moderator, so to speak.

Buddha is somewhat desolate, too spacious. It is like visiting a campsite where only the stones from old campfires are left. There's a sense of its having been inhabited for a long time, but for the time being, no one is there. The inhabitants were not killed; it wasn't a violent move—they just had to leave the place. It's like the caves where Indians used to live, or like the caves in France with the prehistoric paintings. There is a sense of the past, but at the same time it has no particular characteristics. It is very dull, quite possibly in the plains, very flat. Buddha is connected with the color blue. Buddha family art is simple and unobtrusive. It is very direct, but very simple. The buddha family artist tends to use a medium that is heavy and the color black or blue.

Vajra is the sense of sharpness, precision. The color of vajra is white. It is cold and desolate, because everything has to be analyzed in its own terms. Vajra expression deals with objects on their own merits. It never leaves any space, never neglects anything. Vajra is winter, white, austere. Black and white. For example, the ground has its own way of freezing, and trees and plants have their way of freezing. The ground carries the snowfall in a distinctive way. Trees, on the other hand, have an entirely different way of carrying snow, depending on whether their leaves have fallen off or they are evergreens. Vajra is very cold and desolate, but it is also sharp and precise. It requires a lot of focusing.

Vajra is the cold and desolate winter landscape, but less hostile than the karma family. Ingmar Bergman's movies are very vajra. He gets the all-pervasive winter quality, the sharp quality like a winter morning, crystal clear, icicles sharp and precise. But it's not completely desolate; there are lots of things to be intrigued by. It's not empty, but full of all sorts of thought-provoking sharpness. Vajra is connected with the east, the dawn, the morning. It has a sharp silver quality, the morning-star quality.

Vajra art is white, with maybe a suggestion of gold or blue. Sculpturally, it would be metallic, possibly aluminum. It could be destructive art, like a machine built in such a way that it destroys itself—the machine goes beep, beep, beep and then just does its number. If it is painting, it is waterlike and not necessarily representational.

Ratna is related with autumn, fertility, richness. It is richness in the sense of pure restlessness. Trees must bear fruit to be an orchard, for instance. When the fruit is ripe and completely rich, it automatically falls to the ground asking to be eaten up. Ratna has a kind of giving-away quality. It is luscious and extraordinarily rich and open.

Ratna has the quality of midmorning. It is very colorful, but predominantly yellow, connected with the sun's rays and with gold. Whereas vajra is connected with crystal, ratna is connected with the richness of gold, amber, saffron. It has a sense of depth, real earthiness rather than texture. In comparison, vajra is purely texture and has a crispy quality rather than fundamental depth. Ratna is very solid and earthy, but it is not as earthy as buddha, which is dull earthy, uninteresting earthy. Ratna is earthy because it is rich. It is ripe and earthy, like a gigantic tree that falls to the ground and begins to rot and grow mushrooms all over it and is enriched by all kinds of weeds growing around it. There is a sense that animals could nest in that big log. Its color begins to turn yellow, and its bark begins to peel off to show the inside of the tree, which is very rich and very solid and definite. If you decided to take it away and use it as part of a garden arrangement, it would be impossible because it would crumble, fall apart. It would be too heavy to carry, anyway.

Ratna is very rich, yellow, gold. Ratna painting tends to be the least successful, because people overdo it, like a portrait on gold or an overdone flower. Ratna art should be rich, crisp, and powerful; dignified, opulent, and regal.

Padma is connected with the color red and with the spring season. The harshness of winter is just about to become softened by the expectation of summer. Even the harshness of ice is softened when snowflakes begin to become soggy snowflakes. It is the meeting of the two seasons, so it has a half-way-through quality. From that point of view, spring is quite unlike autumn, which has definite qualities of ripening and developing things.

Padma is very much connected with facade. It has no feeling of solidity or texture but is purely concerned with colors, the glamorous qualities. Padma is concerned with output rather than input. In regard to its health or fundamental survival, padma is not concerned with a survival mentality at all. Thus it is connected with sunset. The visual quality of a reflection is more important than its being, so padma is involved with art rather than science or practicality.

Padma is a reasonable location, a place where wildflowers can grow, a perfect place to have animals roaming about. It is like a highland plateau in Tibet at lambing season, with lambs prancing about and eating wildflowers. There are herbs; it is filled with thyme. Padma is a place of meadows. There are gentle rocks, not intrusive, suitable for young animals to play among.

Padma is often misinterpreted as sweet or beautiful, like pop art or Indian posters, kind of overdecorated with beauty and seductive. But that seems to be misleading. True padma art is very luscious and colorful, absolutely brilliant color. It also has curves and shapes. One stroke of color doesn't make your mind interested in it, but padma art has curves, like a lotus.

Karma, strangely enough, is connected with summer. It is the efficiency of karma that connects it with summer. In summer everything is active, everything is growing. There are all kinds of insects, all kinds of discomforting things, all kinds of activities going on, all kinds of growth. During the summer, there are thunderstorms and hailstorms. There is a sense that you are never left to enjoy the summer; something is always moving in order to maintain itself. It's a bit like late spring, but it is more fertile, because it sees that things are fulfilled at the right moment. The color of karma is green. The feeling of karma is like after sunset: late in the day, dusk, and early night. Whereas ratna has tremendous confidence, the karma of the summer is still competing, trying to give birth.

Karma art is the worst, demonic and black. A black panther is an example of karma art. It is not destruction alone, but more like trying to understand the meaning of a thundercloud. The cloud that comes before a thunderstorm has a quality of potential destruction or threat.

The five buddha families are associated with colors, elements, landscapes, directions, seasons—with any aspect of the phenomenal world, as well as describing people's individual styles. In describing people's styles, each family is associated with both a neurotic and an enlightened style. The neurotic expression of any buddha family can be transmuted into its wisdom or enlightened aspect. Buddha neurosis is the quality of being spaced out rather than spacious. It is often associated with an unwillingness to express oneself. Another quality of buddha neurosis is that we couldn't be bothered, we just sit there. The neurotic expression of vajra is anger and intellectual fixation. If we become fixated on a particular logic, the sharpness of vajra can become rigidity. In the neurotic sense, the richness of ratna manifests as being completely fat, extraordinarily ostentatious. We expand constantly and indulge ourselves to the level of insanity. Padma neurosis is connected with passion, a grasping quality, a desire to possess. We are completely wrapped up in desire and want only to seduce the world, without concern for real communication. The neurotic quality of karma is connected with jealousy, comparison, and envy. There are also five wisdoms that go with the five families. Buddha wisdom is all-encompassing spaciousness. Vajra wisdom is clear and precise, like reflections in a mirror or reflecting pool. Ratna wisdom is equanimity; it is expansive, extending. Padma wisdom is discriminating, seeing the details of things. Karma wisdom is the automatic fulfillment of all actions.

You could work with the five buddha family principles by picking up a piece of stone or a twig and approaching it from each of its five different aspects. With each family, a whole different perspective will begin to develop. At that point, you have limitless resources. You don't feel obliged to produce ever more materials, because you can take one thing and make it vajra, karma, padma, ratna, or buddha. You can make all kinds of tartan plaids out of that.

Nobody's World

There are three types of perception: the sense of experience, the sense of emptiness, and the sense of luminosity. With those three levels of perception, we are able to see all the patterns of our life. Whether the patterns of our life are regarded as neurotic or enlightened, we are able to see them very clearly.

In relating with the world, there are some very tough questions: what is the world, whose world is it, and what does relating mean? The basic point is that this is nobody's world, since there is nobody as such. The energy that is constantly taking place does not belong to anybody but is a natural, organic process. Nevertheless, we function as if the world does belong to us, as if I have myself, as if I do exist. From this point of view, the nonexistence of ego—that primordial state of thisness or solid fixation—is not a philosophical matter, but simply a matter of perception. Perception is unable to trace back its existence to its origin. So each perception becomes sheer energy, without a beginner of the perception and without substance—just simple perception.

Perception can be categorized into three levels: experience, emptiness, and luminosity. At the first level, experience, perception is not meaningful self-confirmation, but the experience of things as they are. White is white and black is black. There is a kind of exuberant energy that goes along with the perception. You actually experience something as though you were it. You and the experience become almost indivisible when you experience something in that way. It's that kind of direct communication without anything between.

The second level is the perception of emptiness, which is the absence of things as they are. That is, things have their space; they always come with a certain sense of room. Despite the complexities or the overcrowdedness of our experience, things provide their own space within the overcrowdedness. Actually, that is saying the same thing: overcrowdedness *is* room, in some sense, because there is movement, dance, play. Things are very shifty and intangible. Because of that, there is a very lucid aspect to the whole thing.

The third level of perception is luminosity. Luminosity has nothing to do with any visually bright light but is a sense of sharp boundary and clarity that does not have a theoretical or intellectualized reference point. It is realized on the spot, within the spaciousness. If there were no space, it would be unfocused; there would be no sharpness. But at this third level, in terms of ordinary experience, we have a sense of clarity and a sense of things as they are seen as they are, unmistakably.

So there are three types of perception: the sense of experience, the sense of emptiness, and the sense of luminosity. With those three levels of perception, we are able to see all the patterns of our life. Whether the patterns of our life are regarded as neurotic or enlightened, we are able to see them very clearly. That seems to be the beginning of a glimpse of the mandala perspective and the beginning of a glimpse of the five buddha family energies.

The five buddha energies are not bound to the enlightened state alone; they contain the confused state as well. The point is to see them as they are: thoroughly confused, neurotic, and painful, or extraordinarily pleasurable, expansive, humorous, and joyous. So we are not trying to remove what we perceive, particularly, and we are not trying to reshape the world in the fashion we'd like to see it. We are seeing the world as it is, without reshaping. And whatever comes along in us is a part of the five buddha family principles and the mandala setup.

I would like to remind you that this is a purely experiential approach. We are not talking about philosophy: "Does this thing exist or not?" "Is this a conceptual-level phenomenological experience?" We are not talking about such things. In many cases, the philosophers have gone wrong, so to speak: they have tried to find out the truth about things as they are without experiencing what things as they are might be at the perceptual level. With that approach, we find ourselves completely theorizing the whole thing, without actually knowing what experience we might have.

If we begin to theorize about the existence of the world, its solidity, its eternity, or whatever, we are blocking out a very large chunk of our experience. We are trying to prove too much and trying to build a foundation too much. We are concerned with the solidity of the foundation rather than with its relationship to earth. That seems to be the wrong approach, even to metaphysics. But in this case we are not talking about metaphysics. This is the experiential level, that which we experience in our everyday lives. Such experience doesn't have to be confirmed by theory or by proof. It does not depend on anything of that nature. Instead, it is just simply a matter of everyday life experience from minute to minute. It does not involve any long-term project.

The question of perception becomes very important, because perceptions can't be packed down into a solid basis. Perceptions are very shifty, and they continuously float in and out of our life. You might say, "I have seen a beautiful formation of clouds over the Himalayas," but that doesn't mean that such clouds will always be there. Even though they may be part of the attributes of the Himalayas, you wouldn't expect that when you went to the Himalayas you would always see such beautiful clouds. You might arrive there in the middle of the night under completely clear skies. The idea is that when you describe an experience and relay it to somebody else, whatever you perceive at that moment sounds extremely full, vivid, and fantastic. Somehow you manage to relay the experience of the moment. But if you try to recapture the whole thing or to mimic it, it is impossible. You might end up philosophizing, going further and further from the realities, whatever they might be.

There's a sharp precision that exists in our life, which generally arises from some form of training or discipline, the sitting practice of meditation in particular. It's not that meditation sharpens our perceptions, but that sitting practice makes it possible to perceive. It's a question of removing the clouds, rather than recreating the sun. That seems to be the whole point. An experience of reality may seem to be very uncertain and very faint, but however faint it may be, it still is sharp and precise and tends to bring a lot of clarity.

On the whole, such precise perception depends on a level of watchfulness. Watchfulness is not being careful or tiptoeing about; rather, watchfulness is experiencing a sudden glimpse of something without any qualifications—just the sudden glimpse itself. That has become a problem or an enigmatic question. We ask, "A sudden glimpse of what?" If we have nothing to say regarding what it is, then the whole thing must be absurd. But if we could change our thinking style entirely and open our minds toward something slightly more than what we have and what we have been taught, then we could step beyond that level where everything is based on business transactions and profit making. There is a possibility of awareness without any conditions. From this point of view, *conditions* means anything you use to get out of the awareness or steal from it. So awareness without conditions is just simple, straightforward awareness of itself, awareness being aware without putting anything into it.

That kind of perception seems to be the only key point. It is the key perspective or microscope that is able to perceive the three types of perceptions. At that level, the mandala spectrum and the five buddha family principles are no big deal. They are not extraordinary things to perceive, but matter-of-fact. The basic mandala principle becomes very simple: it is that everything is related to everything else. It is quite simple and straightforward.

Choiceless Magic

We are ready for a firsthand account of what's going on, rather than just listening to stories. Whether we are going to be in Jerusalem next year, the next seder, tomorrow, or the next hour doesn't really matter—the only thing that matters is whether Jerusalem exists now, at this very moment.

I would like to discuss the question of magic. Different perspectives on the world make for different understandings of the functioning of phenomena. That seems to be a natural problem or natural working basis. From that basis, we try to find some common ground in which we could work together, by relying on basic principles such as body, speech, and mind; white, black, red, blue, green; heaven and earth; and all the rest of it.

Those personal expressions that take place in our life, like falling in love or being extremely angry with somebody, are fantastic ground to work with. But that ground has not been developed properly and completely. We reject individual fashions of realization, our particular styles. And on that basis, we try to reject or accept the potentiality and possibilities of being suckered into spiritual trips of all kinds.

People say we are all one and talk about the universality of power. But all that is an expression of frustration, based on not being able to accept their individuality. Because of that, they would like to conform themselves to some large body. When poets are having difficulty creating a poem, they write about the sun and the moon, the earth, or national disasters, things that are seemingly somewhat common. But it is very difficult to get hold of one's individuality; people find that very difficult. Spiritually or otherwise, we do not trust our individuality, and that is one of our biggest problems. We would prefer a monolithic figure, a monolithic governing principle. We use theistic terms like "Our Maker," to refer to one person, one big granddaddy. And if we have problems relating to that person, we should try harder; we must not give up.

The problem with that approach is that our individuality is completely neglected. That doesn't mean we should indulge our personal trips, but there should be some awareness that we are all different. We are all basically, intrinsically different. Our fathers, mothers, children, and great-great-grandparents are different from us, and we are even different from ourselves, from that point of view. So there is an awareness of individuality.

Whenever there is a break from conventionally accepted channels of thought, we get frightened. If we break the law, for example, we might be put in an extremely unpleasant situation psychologically or physically. We do not accept our individuality. We would prefer to have a pre-prepared menu or a travel guide so that we could take the journey without being hassled by our own individuality. But that is problematic: with that approach, magic cannot exist. We simply try to relate with some common factor, the general principles given to us. And we have our ideas of this and that, so we might be included and our ideas proclaimed as part of the categories in that general statement, rather than applying to us. There's a lot of cowardice taking place. That seems to be a general problem with our state of mind, state of being.

Individuality is quite tricky. When individuality exists, as what we are, there is a sense of confusion, uncertainty, and chaos. But there's more room to explore the world and experience the given world and its relationship to ourselves personally. We are individual entities who express reality in our own ways. When you see white, it may not be the same white as the editors of my life assume you should perceive as white. And when you see red, it is the same thing. From that point of view, nobody has the right to commit you to the loony bin if your perceptions don't fit into the general categories according to the books. There is a lot of room for that kind of perspective.

Perceptions are not governed by one statement alone, but by individuals reacting to the basic elements. When individuals react to air, water, fire, space, or earth, they have different responses. Individually, they have different perspectives on all that. Those differences do not become uniform at all—they are ongoing. The magic lies in that individuality. We are relating individually to all kinds of basic things in life that we seemingly share. But we have no idea, exactly. None of us has had a chance to tell each other precisely what our perception of water is like. We could use all kinds of words and ideas and concepts and terms, but that still would not make it clear. They would be somebody else's concepts.

When great artists leave their works of art behind—writings or pictures or music—we feel we are in contact with such people, but we actually have no idea. If they were to come back to life, they might be insulted or even horrified by our understanding of their work. So the spark, or magic, lies in individuality, rather than uniformity. It is not that we count down to zero and then levitate all together, or turn the world upside down. That would be a comic-strip version of magic. And if a group of individuals commit themselves to an organization, and suddenly everybody gets high, turned on, that is like a living comic strip. It's very funny, but there's a great neglect of individuality.

In many cases, we try to avoid our individuality and instead emulate something else. That is a big problem. Individuality sometimes comes out of ego, like wanting to be an emperor, a king, or a millionaire. But individuality can also come from personal inspiration. It depends on the level of one's journey, on how far you have been able to shed your ego. We all have our own style and our own particular nature. We can't avoid it. That would be like asking Avalokiteshvara, who is the embodiment of the padma principle of compassion, suddenly to become a ratna person. The enlightened expression of yourself is in accord with your inherent nature.

The same principle applies to your experience of your own life, in terms of visual perception and your understanding of iconography. There is a basic iconographic pattern in the universe, like the existence of the seasons and the elements, but how we react to that is individual. The path of buddhadharma does not try to unify everything and reduce everyone to good little tantric robots. The intent is to heighten individuality, but within the framework of some common world. Such a framework is actually very questionable at this point, although it performs in that way. In the end, all barriers are broken through and bondages annihilated. At that point, there is room for *that* and *this* to be one. But that takes a lot of steps, a lot of time, effort, and discipline.

The phenomenal world is your own world. Therefore, we cannot say that this phenomenal world is always predictable, that when I see blue you must also see blue. Maybe your sense of blue is more like my sense of red. It could seem that we are agreeing: "Oh, yes, that's a blue light. This one is a red light." But who knows? Nobody knows. So let us not make the psychological assumption that everything is secure. Perceptions are entirely different from this point of view, much beyond the level of seeing blue or not. I know this idea is very frightening and threatening—but let it be threatening. Even your version of being threatened may be entirely different from my version of being threatened. We might be using the same word but in the final realization come up with completely different ideas. There is no point in comparing our worlds. No reference point is necessary. That seems to be simply wasting our energy.

I am afraid what we are discussing is rather dull. It is not quite the same as taking a journey to Peru and seeing the Indians in the Andes or visiting the Tibetans in the Himalayas. Such things have an extra kick, like opium. But we have got to get back to basics sooner or later—the sooner the better. The more entangled we get, the more problems we find. It is like an ingrown toenail: as the nail grows into the toe more and more, finally the whole leg has to be amputated. We don't want to get to that point, so an early warning is best—years ahead, rather than five minutes. Such an early warning system is the duty of somebody who speaks for the teachings.

Getting back to this world of ours, it is not particularly attractive, exciting, and fantastic. It's okay, or maybe it is terrible; I can't speak for everyone. But on the whole, this world is a very anxious one. Whether you are happy or sad, whether you are exuberantly joyful or miserable, it's still an anxious world we're living in. According to Buddhist tradition, anxieties can be transformed into mindfulness and awareness. Anxiety itself can be a reminder, a nudge that keeps waking us up again and again. It's up to us whether we try to get rid of that reminder and make everything smooth, beautiful, and fantastic, or whether we try to make the world into a training ground to learn more, which I suggest is preferable.

We are working with iconography as a journey, rather than as entertainment or excitement or cultural fascination. In attempting to understand iconography, one possibility is to view the whole thing as very sacred. If we manage to see all the little details, we might be saved some day, because the merit of what we see could be a source of deliverance. Another possibility is that by understanding iconography, we might be able to figure out the psychological geography of the Buddhist tradition of how to develop freedom. But both of those approaches seem to be a waste of time. We are not talking about merit or freedom, but about personal experience—how we can actually see this world, how we can live better, if you like. It is not so goal oriented, but it is about how we can live properly right now. How can we live our lives with all the garbage and rubbish that exist around us, amid all kinds of hustle and bustle and threats on our life, hassled by our kids and our parents, threatened by rent problems and money problems? How can we make all that into visual dharma? That seems to be the point. So visual dharma does not mean making everything fantastic, but making something actually happen. It is not a greater Disneyland. By the way, I think Disneyland is one of the best things America has produced. It shows the mirage quality of life and the many different ways one can be amused and entertained. People go to Disneyland and take it very casually, as a day off. "We are doing something for the kids." That's not true; you do it for yourself. It's just like Sesame Street—the parents watch it more than the kids do.

Magic in this case is power. Not power over others, but power beyond "over others." It is the power within oneself. You have enough strength and exertion and energy to view things as they are, personally, properly, and directly. You have the chance to experience the brightness of life and the haziness of life, which is also a source of power. The fantastically sharp-edged quality of life can be experienced personally and directly. There is a powerful sense of perception available to you. And it is realistic, as far as your notion of reality goes. You begin to find some footholds or stirrups, so you can ride and climb much better, so that when you climb a mountain you are not committing suicide. And you don't distort the teachings through little twists of logic. It applies to you personally and it actually works. In contrast, the magical power of a magic show is purely a children's game, in which we only want to prove that some kind of supernormal power exists. Maybe it does and maybe it doesn't, but that approach seems to be for the birds.

The visual setup is always unique, shifty. It's not that visual objects themselves shift, but the individual perceiver's mind shifts constantly. So the whole thing has to be clipped together. Some of those visual shifts become deadly ones—black magic, if you'd like to call it that. If you take the attitude of self-destruction and ego, then visual or auditory perception becomes destructive because your relationship to it is based on your aggression. But that aggression bounces back on you, and you yourself become the victim. On the other hand, visual perception can be creative and open, the most powerful perception of all. It can be realistic and powerful and clear. And when extreme clarity takes place, that also brings a sense of humor.

When you click in to the iconography of the cosmos, you are able to experience a sense of reality that does not depend on reinforcement. You don't have to ask your neighbor, "Am I seeing reality?" The experience is unconditional. Nobody has to confirm your experience—you can confirm it yourself. If you confirmed yourself constantly, heavy-handedly, that would be like incest, but in this case, the self-confirmation is just right. It's like sipping, tasting, swallowing, and digesting properly. This is the visual and auditory perceptual world of magic we experience.

It is not true that there is no magic these days, that we are in the dark ages. A lot of people say that we are too late, we have lost our chance, so we need to wait for some savior to turn up. The only thing we can do is hope for something in the future or emulate people from the past, since presently nobody is getting into anything at all and the whole world has become flat. A lot of people are frustrated; therefore, they have to say such things. It is quite true for them; they are speaking on their own behalf. Such people say that enlightenment has not existed since the time of the Buddha. These days nobody attains enlightenment. And some people say that the next enlightenment plague might take place in another five hundred years, but not now. So the only thing we can do now is pray to be reborn at the right time. We'd better be good boys and girls in order to be candidates for that.

A similar approach, of either a past orientation or a future orientation, takes place in Christianity. But somehow, that whole approach is becoming old hat. Gimmicks are invented right and left to convince us, but we are not quite convinced. We are ready for a firsthand account of what's going on, rather than just listening to stories. Whether we are going to be in Jerusalem next year, the next seder, tomorrow, or the next hour doesn't really matter—the only thing that matters is whether Jerusalem exists now, at this very moment! This is not an emergency, but having a sense of precision. It is a direct understanding that this world of ours is not a future-oriented world or a past-oriented world. It is neither that once we've been saved this world is going to be ours, nor that if we become like past good people, we will have the privilege of using their leftovers. This world of ours is personal, real, and direct. Iconography exists in that real world, which seems to be the most magical one of all.

The only magic that exists is this life, this world, the particular phenomena we are all experiencing right this moment. Right now, right here, you are in this magic. For instance, in giving this talk, I am a captive speaker and you are a captive audience. We can't just walk out in the middle of a sentence—if we were to try to do that, the implications would linger with us for a long time. So we cannot wipe out our past, present, or future. Magic is direct and personal and lingers in our state of being. It is choiceless magic.

One Stroke

Flower arranging and making a brushstroke are unique and absolutely real.
You could actually sum up the history of your life in one stroke—that's possible.

Individual expressions are cultural expressions at the same time. But to begin with, you really have to understand culture. Otherwise it would be like showing a grandmother how to suck an egg or, as we say in Tibet, trying to teach Karmapa the alphabet. A big problem in this country is that people think culture is outside of them. You have American culture, you have a man on the moon, and all kinds of things that are not you but are cultural. Eating hamburgers and hot dogs is cultural, but you personally may not like them. We have been distorting the distinction between ourselves and culture in this country. But truly speaking, culture is a personal experience; culture is made out of a lot of people, all behaving the same way. Everybody wears shirts and pants, and everybody has a zipper in his fly. That is a cultural thing—but at the same time it's personal: you need that zipper to zip up! So we really can't separate cultural and individual from that point of view, particularly in a work of art. You might paint something Americanized; somebody else might paint something Oriental, but the Oriental and Occidental distinction doesn't apply at this point. Culture is how you behave, how you've been told to behave: the transmission from your parents and your friends and how you carry that out. So a work of art cannot be said to be purely cultural or purely individual.

There are two distinct types of Buddhist art, we could say quite safely: that which is purely cultural and that which is basically noncultural. The purely cultural includes ancient sculptures and paintings and architectural designs based on traditional themes. Traditional Buddhist art originated in India at the time of Emperor Ashoka. It includes Chinese and Japanese Buddhist art, Southeast Asian art, and Tibetan art, which is basically an amalgamation of Indian classical art with some Chinese elements. But no matter which country it is from, or whether it is modern or ancient, traditional Buddhist art is much the same in its approach, although the cultural expressions vary. Basically it depicts the Buddha or various types of buddhas, the various lifestyles of the Buddha and other great teachers and their social setups, honoring teachers by means of different thrones, different foregrounds, and different backgrounds. The teachers are surrounded by various disciples, who are equally highly thought-of people, by flying goddesses, and by animals roaming quietly in the background. The sun and moon are shining, and so forth.

The second type of Buddhist art, which developed out of those traditional forms, is basically noncultural. It is a direct aesthetic expression of meditation and devotion. Some sense of faith and trust can be presented in such works of art. For instance, at the Ajanta and Ellora caves in India, built during the reign of Emperor Ashoka, a freestanding temple was built from a huge rocky mountain: the mountain was carved out into rooms and doorways and pillars. It was not particularly meant to be monumental, but it was built functionally. Seeing a gigantic rocky mountain as material to carve temples and statues out of is something like seeing a sheet of paper or canvas in front of you as material to make pictures out of. But the inspiration seems to be at a different level. Nowadays people's inspiration is smaller. If somebody wanted to carve a whole mountain into a temple, people would obviously regard that person as being on a trip, not only because of the costs, but also because of the unreasonability of such an idea. However, I don't think that is a sign of degeneration, particularly. We mustn't think of ourselves as less enlightened and the people of those days as more enlightened. I think it is a cultural change. The human world is becoming more refined, in the sense that we pay more attention to comfort and luxury. We are becoming less hard, and the things around us are easier to handle. Nevertheless, that monumental aspect of art is always present in the noncultural approach. And that noncultural approach to art comes from the sitting practice of meditation.

Once the practice of meditation is developed and you begin to see yourself clearly, then you also begin to see your environment clearly. You don't have to be labeled an artistic person, necessarily; anyone can work on that kind of perception. The only obstacles are hesitation and disinterest. The sitting practice of meditation allows a sense of solidness and a sense of slowness and the possibility of watching one's mind operating all the time. Out of that, a sense of expansion slowly begins to develop and, at the same time, the awareness that you have been missing a lot of things in your life. You have been too busy to look for them or see them or appreciate them. So as you begin to meditate, you become more perceptive. Your mind becomes clearer and clearer, like an immaculate microscope lens.

Out of that clarity, various styles of perception begin to develop, which are the styles of the five buddha families. So artistic expression develops from meditation. To be an artist, one needs mental training through the practice of meditation. That mental training automatically brings with it physical training. That is, when the mind begins to function in a more relaxed way, that is reflected in one's body. Then one begins to develop a sense of humor and appreciation as well. With such clarity, nothing can be distorted.

We're always fascinated with something in the beginning, and we would like to cultivate that fascination and brew it and drink it until we get intoxicated. That is an obvious problem. In order for art to be certain and definite and workable, I would say that you definitely need sitting practice as basic pre-art training. It's the only way to make sure that you don't distort. Nowadays, students don't have an apprentice-teacher relationship with a great master artist. You may study with somebody, take a course, but that person doesn't live with you and work with you throughout your growth. Because of that lack, the only way to become an artist is to meditate a lot. Then you begin to develop a sense of continuity, a sense of dignity and mindfulness.

You could express that dignity and mindfulness in whatever you do, but in a work of art the whole thing is very condensed. For instance, flower arranging and making a brushstroke are unique and absolutely real. You could actually sum up the history of your life in one stroke—that's possible. In your life in general, you never make such a comment as you make in one stroke of the brush, in one flower arrangement, or in one line of poetry. Those are actual statements. They are not very important on their own, but for what they represent. As such, they are very strong and powerful.

When we first perceive things, everything is uncertain. Because of that, we tend to refer back to subconscious preconceptions. That's precisely what preconception is: before we perceive something, we already have some idea.

99

So in viewing the world, we rely on preconceptions. That is also how we begin to create a picture. And once that happens, we begin to feel very confident: "Oh boy, now I have something to work on. Finally I am saved. Phew!" Usually people don't like to show their initial blankness. Particularly people who are highly trained or have studied too much philosophy or have become too involved with the professional world would like to hide that blankness. But that blankness is the basic ground.

Genuine inspiration is not particularly dramatic. It's very ordinary. It comes from settling down in your environment and accepting situations as natural. Out of that you begin to realize that you can dance with them. So inspiration comes from acceptance rather than from having a sudden flash of good gimmick coming up in your mind. Natural inspiration is simply having something somewhere that you can relate with, so it has a sense of stableness and solidity. Inspiration has two parts: openness and clear vision, or in Sanskrit, *shunyata* and *prajna.* Both are based on the notion of original mind, traditionally known as buddha mind, which is blank, nonterritorial, noncompetitive, and open.

The Activity of Nonaggression

Nonaggression is the key to life, and to perception altogether. It is how to perceive reality at its best.

Nonaggression is the key to life, and to perception altogether. It is how to perceive reality at its best. Out of that comes the notion of dignity. Dignity is somewhat more than elegance, which could be genteel in fashion. Dignity has a sense of authentic presence: it has authenticity; therefore it has presence. From that authentic presence, which comes out of nonaggression and gentleness, comes action. And from that, what is known as the four actions take place. According to the vajrayana tradition, these four basic actions are called the four karmas. They have to do with our experience of reality and our perception of art altogether—our perception of life, in this case.

The first action has a sense of pure perception without sharp edges. It is related with the color blue, and also related with the circle, as opposed to a square or other shape. The round shape of the circle represents gentleness and innate goodness, which is absent of neurosis. Blue is like a pure sky and represents space. Blue is also related with the air: cold, fresh air. Altogether, being without sharp edges has a sense of seeing the world at its best. This is the first karma, which is the principle of peace, or pacifying.

The second action has a sense of richness. It is usually depicted as a yellow square with sharp corners. The richness and yellowness are related with the earth. Since the earth is always creating boundaries for us, therefore it is depicted as a square. It also has lots of corners, or directions: namely east, south, west, and north. This action has a sense of being, harmony, a well-settled situation. It is the idea of dignity, or in Tibetan, *ziji*. The second karma, enriching, is the intrinsic energy of our state of mind.

The third manifestation of action is usually depicted as a red half-circle. The redness represents the notion of having a connection with the emotions of

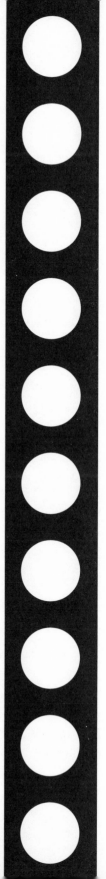

that square earth. So the square earth is not all that square; it has its reference points. As to its being a half-circle, it is a half-circle because it is partly rounded and partly cut off from roundness. There is the fundamental notion of embracing each other: a man and woman embracing or holding hands. For instance, a kiss could be regarded as a half-circle concept—two half-circles meet and therefore make a kiss. It is the concept of passion, but it is not only connected with pure passion in itself; it is also connected with the idea of meeting the mind of another. It is also the idea of daring to let go. The idea is that once there is a sense of richness and of no poverty, we can let go, give away, be generous. This is the source of the third karma, the magnetizing principle.

The fourth action is depicted by a green triangle. It is connected with activity and with destruction. It is green and associated with the strength and power of the wind. Its basic, inherent nature is fearless. A sense of power exists, but the triangle also suggests a very sharp connection by creating three points. That is to say, the meeting of the positive and the negative, as well as the neutral, makes a threesome: therefore, it is a triangle. The notion of balance comes along with that, because if there is too little fearlessness, you might be a coward; and if there is too much fearlessness, everything is too intellectual; so we have a basic point of balance. The triangle is also regarded as representing liberation, or freedom. It is the gate of freedom as to how to perceive reality. So the fourth karma is a heavy one, destruction. It's very simple and clean-cut, as if you were running into a Wilkinson's sword blade. It cuts in all directions. Very simple.

The diagrams representing those four—the blue circle, the yellow square, the red half-circle, and the green triangle—are not regarded as magical or mystical. They are simply regarded as manifestations of how we relate with our lives. If we simplify the color perspective of the four karmas by combining the four colors—blue, yellow, red, and green—into two, the result is lemon yellow and purple. Those two colors were the imperial colors in the courts of China, Japan, Korea, and India, and in the empire of Ashoka as well. Lemon yellow is connected with strength and with the father, or king principle. Purple is considered to be the ultimate feminine, or queen principle. When the masculine principle and the feminine principle are joined to-

:omplishment of all four karmas—pacifying,
:roying. Everything is accomplished in that

_e pacifying, enriching, magnetizing, and de-
_sion of our desire to work with the whole uni-
_ing too eagerly or rejecting too violently; we are
_3uddhism, that freedom is known as the mandala
_ing is moderated by those four activities. In the
_vake; south represents expansion; west represents
_orth represents action. That seems to be the basic
developed

_ifying, is in the east and represents the cooling off of
_sense of peace and coolness, which cools off the bore-
_is. The manifestation of pacifying is gentleness and
The enriching principle, in the south, is basically the
_nd aggression. Arrogance is overcome—it is transpar-
the west, is overcoming poverty. It is free from poverty.
_stroying, is the destruction of laziness. It is in the north.
The idea of _ _ _ ar karmas is not so much how we can handle ourselves,
particularly, but it is how we can handle the whole world. We can actually
operate from this basic mandala principle—in flower arranging, horseback
riding, dishwashing, and all the rest.

State of Mind

Magic lies in the state of mind of the artist. This magic is wakeful magic. The artist's mind is able to tune in to a certain balance or wakefulness—we could call it enlightenment, in fact.

In discussing the state of mind of the artist, we being with attitude. Visual dharma, its application and fruition, is based on the practice of meditation and on Buddhist vision. That does not mean we exclude the visions and the perceptions developed throughout the centuries by artists without a Buddhist background. However, in visual dharma, training one's mind seems to be the key issue. You might be musicians, painters, mathematicians, or photographers, but the principles of visual dharma still apply, to your work as well as to your lives.

Our attitude is the key to discovering the world. Obviously, we have a certain attitude toward ourselves, a certain attitude in relating to others, and a certain attitude in dealing with our world at large. If we haven't developed the right kind of attitude, it is impossible to connect with the world properly. Art involves relating with oneself and one's phenomenal world gracefully. In this case, the word *gracefully* has the sense of nonaggression, gentleness, and upliftedness; that is, a basic attitude of cheerfulness. It is important in becoming artists to make sure that we do not pollute this world; moreover, as artists we can actually beautify the world. Inspired in this way by our contact with dharma art, there is less room for neurosis. That is the actual project of dharma art, which is both necessary and important.

Where things often go wrong is that artists are very poor; and although they might have a lot of talent, intelligence, and vision, they have to struggle to make money. So day by day, hour by hour, their vision goes downhill. In order to make money, they have to relate with perverted, neurotic people who demand that they go along with their particular vision, if you can call it vision at all. So those who commission or underwrite the art and the artist drag each other downhill. It all ends up in a neurotic psychological gutter. In the process you might become a glorious and famous artist, but your work of art is permeated with neurosis and cosmic garbage. In turn, the artistic standard of living of the world begins to go downhill, and we find ourselves living in a very degraded world. Artistic taste does not have to descend to that level of doing clever things to con people and becoming a fundamental con artist.

Our attitude and integrity as artists are very important. We need to encourage and nourish the notion that we are not going to yield to the neurotic world. Inch by inch, step by step, our efforts should wake people up through the world of art rather than please everyone and go along with the current. It might be painful for your clients or your audience to take the splinter out of their system, so to speak. It probably will be quite painful for them to accommodate such pressure coming from the artist's vision. However, that should be done, and it is necessary. Otherwise, the world will go downhill, and the artist will go downhill also.

The artist could take the attitude that to begin with, his or her artwork may not be a money-making venture or popular. But gradually, as you work with your client, your friends, and your audience, they discover that you are a good person. They see that you are genuine, interesting, with a sense of dedication and bravery—and even some arrogance, in the positive sense. Then your world might actually change. The audience and clients may begin to appreciate the way you put yourself into your work, appreciate that your attitude is right. You have actually given birth to an attitude of gentleness and goodness because of your dedication and trueness, so your work rises to a different dimension. At that point, the artist has tremendous power to change the world. The concepts of the world could be changed entirely—visually, audially, and psychologically—by the power of visual dharma.

The second topic is the magic of the artist. In this case, magic doesn't mean that you perform abracadabra in front of your audience or that you suddenly make a million dollars on one painting. Magic lies in the state of mind of the artist. This magic is wakeful magic. The artist's mind is able to tune in to a certain balance or wakefulness—we could call it enlightenment, in fact. At that point, an artist is able to execute masterpieces. There have been examples of that in the past—by artists who were not necessarily Buddhists.

Great paintings have been made, great music composed, and all sorts of arts such as interior decoration and architectural designs executed by people who might not have been great students, technically speaking. So becoming a technocrat is not the way to train to become an artist. First there has to be a sense of vision taking place in one's state of mind. Such vision comes from a state of mind that has no beginning and no end. It is very present, on the spot. We could call that vision first thought–best thought. When that happens, there is no struggle. Anybody could become a genius from that point of view. Everybody has that essence and that possibility. That sense of genius and magic is always applicable.

First thought does not come from subconscious gossip, it comes from before you think anything. In other words, there's always the possibility of freshness. Your mind is not contaminated by neuroses all the time, so there are always possibilities that your whole existence could be good—which it is in any case. Goodness is always there—just catch it on the spot. By cutting through subconscious gossip, you take an attitude of delight in yourself that you are actually doing that. You have a sense of self-existing dignity. Therefore you don't feel so bad. You don't feel loaded with the stuff of your neurosis. So there is a sense of overcoming heaviness and depression. Then you begin to see first thought, which is best thought.

Having developed self-respect and learned a way that you can uplift yourself on the spot, at the level of first thought–best thought, you begin to develop composure and decorum in your state of mind, your body, and your artwork. Composure inspires a sense of richness and beauty, and decorum is a sense of keeping your world together. With decorum, you and your world hang together so well that you do not create any destructive effects or schisms in the phenomenal world, which create further neurotic problems.

If you have both composure and decorum, you have a sense of fully being there, completely being there. You are actually able to cut subconscious gossip, which is the aspect of mind that constantly produces destruction and distractions of all kinds. For instance, when you are about to have a clear vision, a good idea, suddenly there is a gush of wind coming through, which we call subconscious gossip—and that clarity is completely wiped out and destroyed. So it is necessary for us, particularly as artists, to have trust in first thought–best thought. In that way, you will be able to cut through the subconscious gossip that creates doubt and resistance. Such directness is based on training and discipline, being willing to stick with your particular work of art or project until a sense of upliftedness takes place, your dignity develops, and a fresh first thought–best thought emerges.

The dharma artist is not a self-styled artist painting a picture out of his own shit and piss and selling it for a million dollars, but an upright person, a good, gentle, and well-meaning person who is willing to cut through his or her subconscious gossip completely so that a straightforward, brilliant, precise, clear mind takes place. An artist doesn't have to moan and suffer and roll in neurosis all the time. Unfortunately, that perverted version of the artist had evidenced lately, particularly in the Western world. People tend to appreciate those artists who tune in to their particular style of expressing neurosis. They like that neurotic style, so they buy their work of art and cherish it as though they were collecting a pet. Likewise, some people might prefer a three-legged dog for a pet rather than a four-legged dog, because they think it's cute. In that way, art becomes corrupt and decadent, and the whole thing goes down the drain. In contrast, what we are trying to do is produce a work of art, in whatever form we might use, by developing a state of being in which the wakefulness and delight of the Buddhist and Shambhala teachings could be seen and expressed. What that comes down to, again, is one's basic state of mind.

In any perception, first there is the quality of *seeing,* that is, you project out to the world and you see something. That creates a kind of open ground. It also creates possibilities of choosing and rejecting, in the positive sense of discriminating intelligence, as opposed to having our choices determined by emotions such as passion and aggression. You simply see things just as they are. Having *seen,* you can begin to examine the phenomenal world further. At that level, you begin to *look.*

How do you do that? First there's a quality of abruptness—cutting your thoughts, cutting through subconscious mind, cutting any artistic theories altogether. You become just an ordinary individual seeing things at the level, we could say, of cats and dogs. Having *seen,* then you begin to *look* beyond that level and to develop a sense of composure about the whole thing. You actually begin to perceive how the world hangs together. If you want to design something or other, first you see the possibilities of the design; then you can begin to scrutinize and look further. By doing so, you develop a sense of how to appreciate the world of your design and how to manipulate the viewer at the same time—manipulate in the positive sense.

When you *see,* it is first impression. When you *look,* then you conclude what you have seen. Seeing is first thought–best thought, and looking is second thought, maybe best thought. One never knows, it depends on your state of mind. We always see first. Having seen, then our usual selection process, called subconscious gossip, should not be employed. Instead, visual dharma should be employed so we can actually see with a taste, which is looking. That might mean that there is some kind of discrimination, but that's okay. Altogether, what happens is you *see* and then you *look*—and having seen and looked already, then you see again, which is the final conversion. Everything's fine, or maybe terrible—or question mark.

I would like to encourage everybody to practice meditation so we can actually see and look more. If we don't understand ourselves, it will be very difficult to appreciate anything else that goes on in our world. And on the whole, please cheer up. Don't analyze too much.

The next concept is joining the whole thing together and making a statement, which is based on threefold logic. This of course comes from first seeing and looking. Threefold logic is an old Buddhist tradition of how to perceive messages from the phenomenal world, how to appreciate a view completely, and how to present your personal view to somebody else as well.

Threefold logic has to do with presenting a complete world to somebody. Somebody may want you to design a wedding ring or a liquor cabinet or a suit. Somebody might want you to design a whole city or even a nice necklace for their Pekingese dog. Threefold logic can be applied to any situation that comes up. In threefold logic, first we have the ground, then path, and then fruition. It is like holding a fan: first holding the fan, then opening the fan, and then producing a breeze by waving the fan. So threefold logic works in this way: first, one establishes the ground; second, one perpetuates that

ground with a certain logic; and third, one puts all of that together and con-
firms it. That's called threefold logic, and that kind of logic could be used in
designing or producing a work of art. We could describe that as the heaven,
earth, and man principle used in the Japanese tradition of flower arranging,
or as the three bodies of the tantric art of Tibetan vajrayana Buddhism—
dharmakaya, sambhogakaya, and *nirmanakaya.* However they are described, the
three aspects of the background of manifestation, the potential of manifestation, and finally manifesting altogether are very important in order to execute
a work of art.

In the Shambhala tradition, we use the terms *heaven, earth,* and *man.* We
start with the ground, which is heaven. Heaven is not necessarily empty space;
it has the authority of divine principles coming down to earth, as well as a
sense of goodness, gentleness, and togetherness. Heaven has a quality of looking down and a quality of conquering space. There is the sense of being un-
yielding and regal. There is also a playful aspect to heaven. That sense of
openness and room to work could be very dangerous: if you wanted to trip out
on it, the heaven principle could con you into situations. There could be some
self-deception. The blank page is inviting you, asking you to start with your
first dot. So you could start with first mind–best mind and invite a genuine
heaven. That's the basic principle of heaven.

Then we can get into earth, which is a sort of grounded quality, or
mother-earth principle. Pregnant earth, encompassing earth. It could develop
problems with domesticity. Very gentle earth, accommodating everything,
including chaos.

The man principle is quite daring and cute—particularly when they are
babies, though one usually forgets about their diapers. Man has openness and
strength at the same time; there is both daring and goodness. Man is not
necessarily making reference to heaven and earth, but is just an individual
existence, simply taking place.

Then we join them together; and to join heaven, earth, and man, we
need a king. The king principle is not really a fourth logic but is the three of
them brought together to become a unity. If you did not have heaven or sky,
you couldn't exist. But heaven also depends on earth. If there were just heaven
without earth, that would not make much sense; and if there were only earth,

which is the confirmation of heaven, there would be the same problem. And if there were heaven and earth without anybody occupying that space, then nobody would be doing anything at all. Therefore there is man. And at some point all of them join together—not as a fourth principle of logic, but as an extension of the third principle to its logical conclusion. If we have some sense of the dharma of these three principles, then we could put them all together.

Heaven, Earth, and Man

A work of art is created because there is basic sacredness, independent of the artist's particular religious faith or trust.

Dharma art has to do with the state of mind of the artist and how we can communicate that fully to ourselves and to our world. In this regard, we could review the three principles of heaven, earth, and man. Heaven is regarded as space. It provides some psychological space in your state of mind, the sense that there's enough room for you to work. The space of heaven is primordial mind, free from conditions. It is not blank or vacant, but it accommodates everything. It has the quality of wakefulness, the quality of delight, and the quality of brilliance. So the general meaning of heaven is some kind of totality in which we can operate. We can actually walk, dance, kick, and stretch ourselves in that atmosphere. There's lots of room, lots of freedom, and also a sense of wakefulness.

That kind of space becomes an integral part of the process of creation. Restrictions and inadequacies usually come from feeling burdened, as though we are carrying a heavy load. But if we develop the notion of space fully and properly, we begin to find that there is no burden, no load. That is a relief— not just a petty relief, but a larger version of mind altogether. We begin to realize that an extraordinary openness takes place in our lives—in the way we move, the way we eat, the way we sleep, and the way we create a work of art. Tremendous freedom takes place in that basic space. Such freedom is not a product of the creation of art; it is preproduction freedom. That is very important for you to know. Before we produce anything at all, we have to have a sense of free and open space with no obstacles of any kind.

When we have that state of mind, and the right attitude and experience of space has happened already, then out of that comes what is known as blessing, or sacredness. When there's enough sense of space and of no struggle, we can afford to relax. We begin to discover what is known as sacred world, in which any artistic endeavor is regarded as sacred. This is not a product of being smart or clever, whether mathematically, technically, or politically. Sacredness is the binding factor in the heaven principle. If we have one thing here, something else there, and other things arranged all around in our design or visual concept, we don't clutter them all together; and we don't make the big mistake of reorganizing and reproducing our neurosis in the world, because there is a sense of sacredness or blessings. Any good work of art always has that notion of sacredness within it.

Some people look at a painting and think it looks sacred and holy because it invites the sanity of a particular religious tradition. They immediately label it as deriving from Christianity, Judaism, Islam, Hinduism, or Buddhism. But in fact, they regard the artist as having been indoctrinated into a certain faith and therefore able to produce a work of art in accordance with his commitment. I think that way of labeling works of art sacred is sacrilegious. It narrows it down too much, cutting out the whole aspect of human dignity. Basically, it is simply saying that a person who is relatively fanatic in his or her religious commitment will produce the best neurotic art according to that religion. That is a terrible thing to say, absolutely terrible. We are trying to go beyond that narrow sense of sacredness. A work of art is created because there is basic sacredness, independent of the artist's particular religious faith or trust. That sacredness is the heaven aspect, which creates an umbrella, so to speak, that becomes very powerful and very *real*. At that point, human dignity is more important than the particular religion or discipline a person came from. That sounds great, don't you think? Sacredness from that point of view is the discovery of goodness, which is independent of personal, social, or physical restrictions.

The second principle is earth, which has three categories. The first category is *absence of neurotic mind*. The artist produces a work of art on the spot. So whether the artist is sane in the long run or has a larger vision of things or not, each moment there are on-the-spot moments of sanity, connected with the healthiness of the artist's state of mind and his or her relationship to the medium and the work of art itself. According to the Buddhist tradition, neurosis refers to that state of mind which fixates and holds on to things. It is broken down into three categories: passion, which is too gooey, too much glue; aggression, which is too sharp, too threatening, too rejecting; and ignorance, which is a state of stupor that cannot discriminate left from right or black from white. Basically, we're talking about the absence of that, the absence of neurotic mind.

The second category of the earth principle is *thorough relaxation and wholesomeness.* That sense of relaxation is so thoroughly developed in your state of mind and body that as an artist you begin to develop tremendous softness. Your relationship to the world becomes very soothing. It is so soothing that before you create a work of art, you might feel as if you had gone through a washing machine. You are completely relaxed and you just flop. Your mind and body are so mixed together that a sense of goodness is already taking place in you. You could say it's like coming out of a sauna bath: you feel so relieved to come out of that room, and a sense of relaxation takes place. So basically we are talking about relaxation. Another school or philosophy of art might say that if the artist were aggressive and neurotic enough, on the spot that would produce a wonderful work of art. But to our way of thinking, from the visual dharma point of view, it is just the opposite. A person has to experience relaxation before producing a work of art.

The third category of earth is *absence of laziness.* When you begin your work of art, a certain drive develops, and that drive should be absent of laziness. You might have a great theme that you want to execute, so you have to go on constantly in accord with your vision of what you want to do. If you cut down your full vision and create a work of art at a half-vision level, that is breaking the discipline or morality of artistic endeavor. So there has to be an absence of laziness. In other words, when we want to produce a work of art, we should do it all the way.

Then we have the principle of man, which falls into two categories. Number one is *freedom from subconscious gossip.* If subconscious gossip is going on in your state of mind, if there is that sense of wildness and your mind is constantly filled with thoughts, then it is very hard to execute anything. So that has to be controlled and overcome. The problem there is that you are not relating with either the heaven or the earth principle, so you can hardly create a man principle at all. But wandering mind can be cut through, either before or during your execution of the work of art. In fact, you can use the very process of executing the work of art as a way to cut subconscious gossip, through your commitment to the medium and to the vision that exists in you and in your work.

The second category of the man principle is *absence of regret.* Usually a sense of regret takes place all the time, which is known as artist's fever. Such regret usually relates to the past. But in this case, we are talking about regrets of all kinds: regrets of the future and regrets of the present, as well as regrets of the past. There is a very slick but at the same time very deep-rooted depression taking place, which looks back and forth all the time. With that kind of regret, which is almost remorse, completely obscuring your vision of heaven and earth, you can't produce a work of art at all.

All together, these three principles—heaven, earth, and man—deal with how we can integrate our state of mind into a work of art. A fourth principle, though not exactly the same kind of principle, is that of the universal monarch. It is what joins heaven and earth together. This principle is singlefold: that is, it says that body and mind are able to work together harmoniously. Therefore, the mind develops a sense of openness and peacefulness, and the body develops an absence of speed and aggression. In that way, a work of art becomes gentle rather than contrived or extraordinary. It becomes a good work of art, very genuine, and it becomes worthwhile, really good, to be an artist. You can take a lot of pride in being an artist, in the positive sense. You will be so happy and feel so good to be an artist. You can work according to the principles of heaven, earth, and man, and you can expose yourself by means of those principles. It could be extraordinary, quite fabulous.

Endless Richness

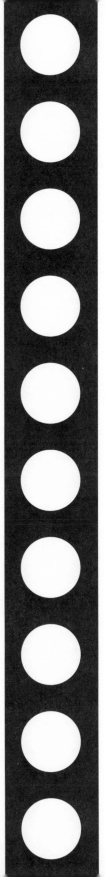

The whole philosophy of dharma art is that you don't try to be artistic, but you just approach objects as they are and the message comes through automatically.

Teaching is not meant to be verbal alone. It is very visual. For instance, a medium such as film rather than converting people to Tibetan Buddhism, can provide virgin territory unadulterated by conventional or institutionalized spirituality for anyone with curiosity or a question in mind. I hope that awake people who question their own basic sanity will find another way of looking into their neuroses without getting just another "answer to their problems."

The whole philosophy of dharma art is that you don't try to be artistic, but you just approach objects as they are and the message comes through automatically. It is like Japanese flower arranging. You don't try to be artistic; you just chop off certain twigs and branches that seem to be out of line with the flow. Then you put the twigs in the container and the flowers underneath, and it automatically becomes a whole landscape. Likewise, when you see a painting by a great artist, it doesn't look as though someone actually painted it. It just seems to happen by itself. There is no gap, no cracks at all—it's one unit, complete.

Creating art is like meditating. You work with one technique for a long, long time, and finally the technique falls away. There's ongoing discipline and continuity, stubbornness. You are willing to relate with it even if the object rejects you or the light isn't right or something else goes wrong. You still go on and do it.

I would like to create a film in such a way that the audience has to take part in it. To do so, we would need to provide lots of space, speed, and richness. Those three principles, properly interrelated, seem to work together so that the audience begins to take part in the presentation. As they watch the screen, they feel they are giving birth to each vision rather than passively absorbing some ready-made creation. There should be room to question, not have the whole thing presented to you like machine-gun fire. The audience should take part in it. To do so, space is the most important thing—space and silence. Then you begin to value objects much more. It is quite possible we might allow too much space, which may not be particularly popular at first. Nobody is going to say, "Wow, how exciting!" It may seem alien at first. But then, when they change gears and see it a second time, next week, next month, it will be different.

When people go to a movie, they go because they want a change. They want something to see besides their usual scene of washing dishes, working in the office, or whatever. This automatically means that they need space. So if a movie presents space, no matter how irritating it may be, it will be worth it. The audience won't come out tensed up; they'll come out relaxed. They will have gone through the whole trip of waiting to see something and then actually seeing something. They will have gone through an eye-massage process. That is a challenge for both the audience and the filmmakers. It is like crossing the Himalayas to escape from the Chinese.

It has been said with relation to *maha ati* practice that the eyes are one of the most important exits. In fact, they have been called the door of *jnana,* the highest wisdom. So visual effects are the most important in their effect on the mind. Generally, an audience comes to see a film with certain expectations. When they begin to feel they are not going to see what they expected, it is somewhat strangling. But at the brink of nothing ever happening, something happens—something quite different from what you expected.

A film should make suggestions rather than feed information. In fact, not giving information is one of the best things we can do to help the audience take part in a film. Once they have been fed, they have nothing else to do but walk out. But if not enough information is given, although indications are there, they have to work on it and think about what has been presented. This whole approach to art is based on putting out just a corner of our knowledge, instead of saying a lot, even though that would make people feel more comfortable and secure.

For instance, if you study with a teacher who acquired his understanding by information alone, that person may tell you very wise things, beautiful things, but he won't know how to handle the gaps. He blushes or he gets embarrassed or he fidgets around between stories, between the wisdoms that he utters. But if you are dealing with somebody who is completely competent, who is actually *living* the information, the teaching has become part of his whole being, so there is no embarrassment. It goes on and on and on, like the waves of an ocean. There is endless richness. You receive a lot, but at the same time you don't feel that he emptied out all his information to you. You feel there's much more to be said.

If you are completely confident in yourself, you don't have to think about the audience at all. You just do your thing and do it properly. You become the audience, and what you make is the entertainment. But that needs a certain amount of wisdom. When an artist does a painting for a commission, there is a good likelihood that his painting will be one-sided because he is aware of the audience, and he has to relate to the educational standards of that audience. But if he presents his own style without reference to an audience, the audience will automatically react, and their sophistication will develop, eventually reaching the level of the artist's.

Any entertainment that aspires to art should not work with the audience like an advertisement. Trying to please the audience lowers the level of sophistication constantly. That's what's wrong with the American marketing system. When you try always to please the audience, you have to produce more and more automatic gimmicks, more and more plastic. Finally, people don't even have to walk out of their rooms to make things work; they just press a button and get entertained.

As artists, we have the responsibility of raising the mentality of the audience. People might have to reach out with a certain amount of strain, but it's worth it. The whole civilization then begins to raise its level of sophistication. It is possible that the first attempt will be a failure. You might not get enough people in the audience to work that way. But gradually they will pick up on it. That has actually been happening. If you relate to yourself properly, then, since there are a lot of people like you, you become a catalyst for the rest of the world. The audience comes to you as to a queen bee. There is less sense of salesmanship or the feeling that you have to con people, so people come to you.

The beautiful thing about Buddhism, if I may say so, is that Buddhists don't try to con you. They just present what they have, say it as it is, take it or leave it. If you try to con people, to make money immediately, it becomes prostitution. When we try to meet the immediate demands of the public in their present state of sophistication, we have to lower our standards constantly, whereas if we allow for some kind of resistance to our work, the audience has to jump up higher and higher. They have to work with their patience and they have to work with their sophistication, so the public automatically gets educated. It's a plot, but a compassionate plot.

People in this country are very awake; they are looking for something—and usually they get the something they expect. But next time, they will be able to get something beyond what they are used to.

Back to Square One

At this point, we are in a very powerful spot: being in the present, we can reshape the whole future. Therefore, shouldn't we be more careful, shouldn't we be more awake in what we are doing this very moment?

Art in everyday life seems to be our destination. The question is, how do we begin? Our main purpose is to develop an understanding of life and art. If we don't have a life of our own, we don't have art of our own, so we end up discussing the question of what is life—which is art, naturally. Life is based on various concepts and ideas, such as life being a big drama, a fantastic showpiece, an absolute torture chamber, or just gray. We have all kinds of ideas about it. But there seems to be a problem when we try to reshape the world. We don't reshape the world haphazardly, of course; we reshape it in accord with our beliefs and our dreams. So the world is reshaped according to our own ideas and the way we want it to be.

The problem with that is that, in the end, the world begins to haunt us back. Because we have reshaped the world, the world begins to demand more and more attention. Since it is our world, what we make of this world, it acts as a mirror. When that happens, a lot of people panic—enormously, to say the least. They begin to feel trapped in their own creation and see it as unjustified, something they didn't deserve. People go so far as to discuss the question of spirituality, the ultimate level of judgment, and the question of being fair to everybody. Everything seems to come back to the psychological, rather than the physical situation that we could do something about at the beginning.

Obviously, we must think first before we do. But the question is more complex: how to think, what to think, why to think, what is "to think"? No one can stop or control your thought process or your thinking. You can think anything you want. But that doesn't seem to be the point. The thinking process has to be directed into a certain approach. That does not mean that

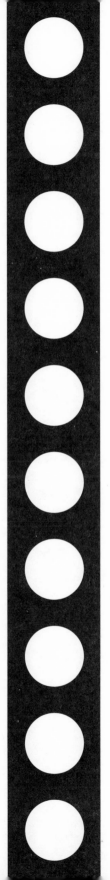

your thinking process should be in accord with certain dogma, philosophy, or concepts. Instead, one has to know the thinker itself. So we are back to square one, the thinker itself: who or what thinks, and what is the thought process?

The thinking process, to begin with, is a confused one. If you really look into the depths of its existence, the whole thing is extraordinarily confused. It is jumbled up with a lot of stuff we have collected throughout our life of birth and death, our existence in our world. The question is, if we work with that, could we produce a work of art? Is there any hope that finally the world will be what is desired or dreamed of as a perfect world, the world that manifests itself as the re-creation of the Golden Age? It's doubtful. At the same time, nobody knows. Nobody experienced an absolute golden age—and even if somebody had created a golden age, it is doubtful whether that would satisfy us. Maybe we would begin to feel that there was a problem with it.

On that basis, how do we begin our world? Up to this point, we have not yet begun our world. However, we are still subjects of the world; we can't avoid that. But from this point onward, since we have not yet begun our world, we are the masters of the world, the creators of the world. We can do whatever we want, whatever we like. Since we can do anything we want, we seem to have a lot of power. So at this point, we are in a very powerful spot: being in the present, we can reshape the whole future. Therefore, shouldn't we be more careful, shouldn't we be more awake in what we are doing this very moment? I think the suggestion would be quite strong that, "Sure, we should." We should do something positive and intelligent or, for that matter, negative and intelligent. As long as there's intelligence involved, there seems to be no problem finding our way through.

The crux of the matter is: what do we do and how do we do it? Do we just sit and wait? Do we read stacks and stacks of books, trying to collect ideas from that? Do we take miles and miles of journeys, trying to meet with supposedly clever, enlightened people and collect information from them? Since we do not know what we are doing, if we do something in that light, it seems to be fruitless. Quite possibly we end up bumping into somebody who is absolutely absurd and getting false ideas about what they have to say. We regard that as our first discovery and begin to mess up our future. Quite possibly, we could collect all kinds of garbage by reading books, and our misunderstanding and partial understanding could create enormous chaos. We could become a walking book, but what happens after that? Another alternative is just to have a good time, go to Florida, California, South America, drink tequila, listen to sweet music. Just forget everything and have a good time.

Somehow none of that is quite what we mean by nowness or being in the now. Nothing seems to be the ideal situation to fill that gap of nowness. Whatever we do, we are involved in some kind of trip, enormous deception. Our sense of boredom led us into entertaining ourselves, or trying to entertain ourselves, and that whole process has become a rat race, a vicious circle. It is constant, with no end, no beginning, purely absurd. Another suggestion might come up, which is to go and practice meditation. Try to raise your consciousness, whatever that may be. Try to imitate holy men and become a holy person. But that seems to be the same thing. So at this point, whatever we do, we can't get out of anything.

We don't seem to be doing anything real. We are constantly trying to mimic that and that and this and this. Nothing is very personal. There's nothing personal and nothing real in terms of our experience. Everything we do is copying something, following something, trying to find new materials to fit our own confused jigsaw puzzle. Somehow not only is that not working, but it is the wrong end of the stick. And if you expect me to give you the answer, that may be very hard to come by. It seems that whenever you have a problem, there is a concrete answer: "Take this pill. Do this." But that approach seems to be founded upon false premises, for the very reason that you find the answer because you are weak. Therefore you are fed by nipples. And if you feel lonely, you play with toys and you have a babysitter: "Let me read you a bedtime story. Let me sing you a lullaby." So we are back to square one.

If you really want to do something properly, if you really want to do it genuinely, we could say quite safely that you have got to be back to square one. You have to taste and experience that. Otherwise, there seems to be a problem with "art in everyday life," as the cliché goes. Any work of art is expressing ourselves in particular terms and concepts. Artistic talent is expressed in media of all kinds. But what is artistic talent? What makes you artistic? What convinces you, if you are uncertain, that a work of art is a real expression of yourself? Or is a work of art something to make sure that the rest of the world is convinced about you, so that in turn you yourself find ground to exist? Such questions have never been looked at or studied properly. From this point of view, genuine artistic talent is experiencing a sense of being back to square one. Being completely bewildered by that, we make our first expression of art in the sense of copying or imitating, tuning in to a philosophy, or spiritual waves. But going beyond that approach, if we feel that we are back to square one and completely bewildered, we have a beautiful white canvas in front of us.

The topic of art in everyday life is not particularly designed for artists. Ordinarily, a good artist needs a lot of ideas, a lot of tricks and concepts. Hopefully, we will not provide that here, for the sake of our sanity. If I do so, I take everything back—what I have said and what I might say. I find myself working in administration, with organizational issues, which involves looking into the economy, aesthetics, and social situations of the groups of people involved. I am also involved with educational decision making of all kinds— and I find the best time for me to make decisions is when my mind is completely blank, when I find myself back to square one. At that absolute, unbiased level of mind, something takes place. I'm not suggesting that might be the trick, and it is not just a story, which could be very fishy. When we are back to square one, we cut all our connections and roots, and at the same time, we appreciate their shadows. Obviously, you still respect your umbilical cord, because you have a tummy button. Nobody has plastic surgery to remove that, and nobody regards it as an ugly mark; it is regarded as an organic expression that you have been born in this world and you have a tummy button.

Back to square one. That seems to be the starting point of any genuine expressions we might express. Genuine expressions have to be self-existing, born within one. So if you are going to express such genuine expressions, you have to get back to genuine ground. And so far as we are concerned, at this point the only genuine ground we have is back to square one.

If you cut all kinds of roots and fascinations, all kinds of entertainment, regarding it as a very subtle form of conmanship, what do you have? You might say, nothing. But it's not quite nothing—it's back to square one. The point is that your genuine existence and expressions should not be colored by any form of artificiality. However subtle, however magnificent, however beautiful or holy it may be, it still discolors your existence. So if you have a sense of ultimate cynicism, you are back to square one. If you see through any trips that are laid on you, or anyone trying to influence you, if you see through how you yourself are influencing somebody else's ideas or borrowing ideas and concepts from somebody else—then you are back to square one. What else do you have, except your square one? It's not difficult; we are constantly back to square one. If we are in the midst of making decisions and not knowing what to do; if we are confused, terrified, or sick—we are constantly back to square one. If we feel extremely weak, not knowing how to proceed to our next strategy, we are back to square one. It is very familiar ground. It is not a particularly extraordinary state of mind, but highly ordinary.

At that point, making a decision may involve a strategy that takes us off square one or a genuine expression coming from square one. It is very personal: sometimes it does; sometimes it doesn't. Take the example of falling in love. The conditions causing you to fall in love with somebody are not because your husband or your wife is a wealthy person, has a lot of intelligence, is a good breadwinner, or would be good for you. If you don't have those accessories and you begin to like somebody as another human being and appreciate him or her as your mate, then you are operating from a square-one point of view; whereas if you have been talked into it by your parents in a matched marriage or through religious concepts, it is operating from square thirty-three. However, if it is genuinely felt and personally experienced, it is like the elements: fire burns, water is moist, air moves, space is spacious.

Basically, square one is your ground. If you're on your own ground, I don't think there is any danger. Usually there's an element of sanity, a seed or essence of sanity operating in you if you are back to square one. There's something positive happening. If you feel that being back to square one is dangerous, that must be another square, not square one.

If you feel confused, you might wind up not doing anything. But actually, not doing anything at all might be healthier than wasting your time doing something. Everything amounts to that, eventually, so I think there's no problem with that. The situation of being cornered is good, if you can use such terminology. It is fruitful, genuinely square one. Unless you are cornered, you don't really do anything much. But once you are cornered, you begin to exercise your sanity and intelligence. That's usually a characteristic of human behavior. I don't think anybody will stand still all that long, afraid to make a move. That nonaction might prove to be an embryonic situation.

Back to square one is more than simply trusting your intuition. We seldom have transparent intuition. Instead, our intuition is very solid and is influenced and colored by all kinds of things, and it is usually conditioned by concepts. Back to square one is simple, straightforward. You feel you've been cornered, and you have to pounce out in one way or another. Not knowing exactly what to do, you feel very vivid about the whole reality around you, and at the same time, you know that you've been cornered. Through the process of paranoia, you have been purified as well; you have been stripped to the waist and downward as well to your toenail and the floor you are standing on. So you have nothing to hide. You are completely transparent; you are cornered. It's more than intuition; it's experienced intuition. Usually the intuitive process is still a kind of radar system, rather than experience. This is much more real in some sense. It is very direct and somewhat extraordinarily penetrating.

You could get yourself into such a square-one situation. In the Buddhist tradition, it's part of the discipline, or path. But it is not a path in the sense of going forward and speeding to your goal. Instead, you are coming backward, getting *into* the whole thing rather than getting *out of* it. And sometimes you find that the rug has been pulled from under your feet; you find yourself back to square one. If you work with that situation—not try to get out of it but sit with it and nurse that experience of immense desert, the desolation of not finding anything to fool around with—then there seems to be something to it, definitely. Square one is where you come back to when you are finally thrown back on your backbone. However, there is a problem if you hear too much about the merits of square-one-ness. It becomes a doctrine again, and it ceases to be square one. At that point, it is something else; we could hardly call it square one.

Genuine square one is when you realize the desolateness, the spaciousness, and all kinds of words we could use for that which is completely devoid of any feedback at all. You are pushed back and punched in the nose—but you are still sitting there cross-eyed, like an owl made out of gold. You are slightly sick because you have finally confronted your good old self, but at the same time, you feel slightly relieved because you can still maintain your existence. That type of square one is primordial, rather than imaginary, or a doctrinally conceived idea or concept. It is the really genuine one. Square one should be devoid of any culture. When you're at a low moment of your energy, completely beaten down to the point of death and it feels like you are a piece of shit, you don't feel any culture about that. You feel very genuinely noncultural—and definitely real.

A sense of nonthinking is necessary at the same time as a sense of the thinking process. According to the Buddhist tradition, the sitting practice of meditation provides basic footing, solid ground to develop further understanding, further experiences of square one. So I feel somewhat guilty if I provide just words, words, words, planting further confusion in the world of confusion; whereas if people sit and stop thinking and talking by means of meditation, I feel that we have planted dynamite to transcend the world of confusion. So it would be good if you could practice meditation as much as you can, as much as is physically and psychologically possible. It would be good if you could get into the sitting practice of meditation. You could become more clear and sane, and you could also influence the national neurosis in that way. Keep that in mind.

If you begin to step out of square-oneness, then you can trip out on all kinds of things. I think it is a problem that artists are not willing to go back to square one. They are unwilling to face their basic situation unless they can find a dramatic message in it. Obviously, people on Madison Avenue appreciate it if artists come out with a dramatic message, which helps in exhibiting their showpieces. But that is not the only world—there are other worlds than Madison Avenue, as we know.

If there is desire, it's easy to portray. But if there is no desire, it's very hard to portray that feeling in terms of visual art. For instance, people have great difficulty portraying the Buddha, because he doesn't do anything. He just sits there. Bodhisattvas, the people who out of compassion took vows to save all sentient beings, are easier to portray. They tend to have a benevolent look, very gentle and soft, and they are supposed to show sorrow and pain because they realize that their fellow sentient beings are in pain and they want to save them.

The question of square one is very important. An artist should not try to get away from his media, which includes his life situation. And for that matter, meditators, who are also artists, should not get away from *their* media: their passion, aggression, and ignorance—whatever goes on in their minds. As long as you try to get away from that and look for alternatives, such as a better future or more pleasant experiences, then you begin to mess up the whole thing. So the issue is keeping your ground, where you came from. You should not be ashamed of that. If you are black, you're black; if you are white, you're white. You cannot get away from it, or have plastic surgery. So it is a question of acceptance. From that point of view, art is the practice of meditation, and meditation is a work of art.

Everybody has their own square one, and they get back to it. That seems to be a universal thing; otherwise, they wouldn't exist. Since everybody does exist, since they have their existence and functions in life, there is the possibility of seeing square one in a more clear and precise way. One is one; it is a number. When you have one, that indicates the possibilities of two and three and four. But that doesn't necessarily mean that you are going to get to square two and the rest of it. Then you have zero, which is not any kind of figure. It denotes nothing, I suppose. We want to be something, right? Even if we are back to square one, we are there, we are something. We don't want to be nothing, and we constantly try to avoid that. That is the problem. So the only alternative—not even alternative, but only choice, so to speak—is to be zero.

So square one is the basic ground from which we function, and square zero seems to be beyond even our functioning. Isness, without any definitions. It is not so much branching out, but branching in. There is still resistance to going back to zero, and it has always been a problem that square one could be the excuse for you not to have to go back to zero. At least you have the number one to clench on to; at least there's that first number you made. You achieved your identity at square one, and that seems to be the problem. So ultimately, one has to return to zero. Then you begin to feel that you can move around. You can do a lot of things, not be numbered. You're not subject to your own numbers, and you are not confined to a pigeonhole. So your situation could be improved if you know you have nothing but zero, which is nothing. There's no reference point anymore, just zero. Try it. It is an expression of immense generosity and immense enlightenment.

Art Begins at Home

Dharma art is not purely about art and life alone. It has to do with how we handle ourselves altogether: how we hold a glass of water, how to put it down, how we can hold a note card and make it into a sacred scepter, how we can sit on a chair, how we can work with a table, how we do anything.

Dharma art is not purely about art and life alone. It has to do with how we handle ourselves altogether: how we hold a glass of water, how to put it down, how we can hold a note card and make it into a sacred scepter, how we can sit on a chair, how we can work with a table, how we do anything. So it is not a narrow-minded approach or a crash course on how to be the best artist and get the best money out of that. I'm afraid it doesn't work like that. Dharma art is a long-term project, but if you are willing to keep up with the basic discipline, you will never regret it. In fact, you will appreciate it a lot and you will be very moved at some point. Whenever you make your breakthrough and develop that reference point, you will appreciate it and enjoy it enormously. You will be so thankful. That is my personal experience. It has been done, and it will be done in the future.

Dharma art is a question of general awareness. It is much more than art alone. For instance, if you are involved with an art form, such as flower arranging, you could begin with your own household, organizing it in that fashion. You could set up a place for flower arrangements. In a Japanese household, there is always a place for a central arrangement, called a *tokonoma.* Or in the Buddhist tradition, there is always a shrine of some kind. Not only that, but you could work with the notion of how you arrange the kitchen, where you put your cups and saucers and where you put your pots and pans, how you put things away and arrange them properly. Also, in the bathroom, where you put your soap, where you put your towel; and in the bedroom, how you fold your sheets. You begin to come into your home with a sense that there is a total household, which takes hard work and discipline. At the same time, it is so elegant and practical that you don't have to run into messy edges of any kind. That seems to be the start.

Once you have your domestic setup properly done, ideally you can invite a few friends to your house and show them how you handle your life. From that you can introduce flower arranging to people. In that way, flower arranging is not just something you do when you are feeling bad, like making a little flower thingy for your mantelpiece; it is a total world. Students should learn that; they should know that. You are not just making flower arrangements in your living room, but you have that same general sense of perception everywhere. So dharma art involves how to rinse your towel in the bathroom, how you hang it up properly so it dries nicely and you don't have to iron it. It has to do with how your sheets are folded, how your table is placed in the sitting room. It is a total world, in which you pay attention to every little detail. If the executive director of IBM came to visit you, and you were fooling with these little things, he might think you were crazy—but on the other hand, he might appreciate you. This approach is not necessarily Oriental; it is just the basic sanity of how you do things properly and have a place for everything. It is running your household as a work of art. That seems to be the main point.

In this case, the particular arrangement of the household is not the duty of the husband or the wife or the children, but everybody does it. They each do their part, so nobody begins to be labeled as the housecleaner or the cook. Everybody in the family should learn how to cook, and they should also learn how to clean up after they have cooked. Everybody should learn how to make things clean and orderly. That way, eventually you won't need a spring cleaning, as they say. Instead of once a year doing a whole big sweep, it's being done every minute, every hour, every day. So everything is being handled properly and beautifully, and you begin to appreciate your home.

Even though you might be living in a plastic-looking condominium or apartment, you can still look elegant. That seems to be the basic point. It's very natural. You don't just throw things on the floor. When you take off your pajamas, you fold them up and put them in their proper place. Dharma art is natural awareness. You do not need to make a special effort or have a chunk of time in order to do a good job. It's just a question of where you place your soap on your dish, how you fold your towel, which doesn't take all that much extra time. That is dharma art, actually. We could experiment with that. Do you think it's possible?

SOURCES

From the Author: July 1974 letter.

Discovering Elegance: Public Talk, Dharma Art, San Francisco, 1981.

Great Eastern Sun: Talk 3, Visual Dharma Seminar, The Naropa Institute, 1978.

Basic Goodness: Talk 4, Visual Dharma Seminar, The Naropa Institute, 1978.

Meditation: Talk 1, Art in Everyday Life, Padma Jong, 1974. Talk 2, Dance of Enlightenment, Padma Jong 1975.

Art in Everyday Life: Talk 10, Vajradhatu Seminary, Jackson Hole, 1973.

Ordinary Truth: Talk 1, Iconography of Buddhist Tantra, The Naropa Institute, 1975.

Empty Gap of Mind: Talk 3, Iconography of Buddhist Tantra, The Naropa Institute, 1975.

Coloring Our World: Talk 2, Iconography of Buddhist Tantra, The Naropa Institute, 1975.

New Sight: Talk 5, Iconography of Buddhist Tantra, The Naropa Institute, 1975.

The Process of Perception: Talk 6, Iconography of Buddhist Tantra, The Naropa Institute, 1975.

Being and Projecting: Talk 4, Mudra Theater Intensive, Rocky Mountain Dharma Center, 1976.

Lost Horizons: Talk 9, Iconography of Buddhist Tantra, The Naropa Institute, 1975.

Giving: Talk 4, Iconography of Buddhist Tantra, The Naropa Institute, 1975.

Self-Existing Humor: Talk 8, Iconography of Buddhist Tantra, The Naropa Institute, 1975.

Outrageousness: Talks 2 and 3, Art in Everyday Life, Karmê-Chöling, 1974.

Wise Fool: Talk 10, Iconography of Buddhist Tantra, The Naropa Institute, 1975.

Five Styles of Creative Expression: Milarepa Film Workshop, Karma Dzong, Boulder, 1972. Talk 2, Art in Everyday Life, Karmê-Chöling, 1974. Chapter 9, *Journey without Goal* (Boston: Shambhala Publications, 1981).

Nobody's World: Talk 4, Mandala of the Five Buddha Families, Karmê-Chöling, 1974.

Choiceless Magic: Talk 7, Iconography of Buddhist Tantra, The Naropa Institute, 1975.

One Stroke: Talk 6, Dance of Enlightenment, Padma Jong, 1975.

The Activity of Nonaggression: Talk 4, Dharma Art Seminar, The Naropa Institute, 1979. Talk 2, Dharma Art Seminar West, Los Angeles, 1980.

State of Mind: Talk 1, Visual Dharma Seminar, The Naropa Institute, 1978.

Heaven, Earth, and Man: Talk 2, Visual Dharma Seminar, The Naropa Institute, 1978.

Endless Richness: Milarepa Film Workshop, Karma Dzong, Boulder, 1972.

Back to Square One: Talks 1 and 2, Art in Everyday Life, Karmê-Chöling, 1974.

Art Begins at Home: Talk 3, Dharma Art Seminar West, Los Angeles, 1980.

PHOTOGRAPHY CREDITS

1. *Photographer unknown. From the collection of Vajradhatu Archives.*

2. *35mm slide by Chögyam Trungpa Rinpoche, 1972. From the collection of Vajradhatu Archives.*

3. *35mm slide by Chögyam Trungpa Rinpoche, 1972–1975. From the collection of Vajradhatu Archives.*

4. *35mm slide by Chögyam Trungpa Rinpoche, 1974. From the collection of Vajradhatu Archives.*

5. *35mm slide by Chögyam Trungpa Rinpoche, 1974. From the collection of Vajradhatu Archives.*

6. *35mm slide by Chögyam Trungpa Rinpoche, 1974. From the collection of Vajradhatu Archives.*

7. *Photographer unknown, 1963. From the collection of Vajradhatu Archives.*

8. *35mm slide by Andrea Roth, 1980. From the collection of Vajradhatu Archives.*

9. *35mm slide by Andrea Roth, 1980. From the collection of Vajradhatu Archives.*

10. *35mm slide by Andrea Roth, 1980. From the collection of Vajradhatu Archives.*

11. *Color print by Herb Elsky, early 1970s. From the collection of Vajradhatu Archives.*

12. *Original print supplied by Gina Stick. Photographer unknown, early 1970s. From the collection of Vajradhatu Archives.*

13. *Robert Del Tredici, photographer, 1980.*

14. *Robert Del Tredici, photographer, 1980.*

15. *Robert Del Tredici, photographer, 1980.*

16. *35mm slide by Chögyam Trungpa Rinpoche, 1974. From the collection of Vajradhatu Archives.*

17. *35mm slide by Chögyam Trungpa Rinpoche, 1974. From the collection of Vajradhatu Archives.*

18. *Liza Matthews. From the collection of Vajradhatu Archives.*

19. *35mm slide by Andrea Roth, 1980. From the collection of Vajradhatu Archives.*

20. *35mm slide by Andrea Roth, 1980. From the collection of Vajradhatu Archives.*

ABOUT THE AUTHOR

Ven. Chögyam Trungpa was born in the province of Kham in Eastern Tibet in 1939. When he was just thirteen months old, Chögyam Trungpa was recognized as a major *tülku,* or incarnate teacher. According to Tibetan tradition, an enlightened teacher is capable, based on his or her vow of compassion, of reincarnating in human form over a succession of generations. Before dying, such a teacher might leave a letter or other clues to the whereabouts of the next incarnation. Later, students and other realized teachers look through these clues and, based on careful examination of dreams and visions, conduct searches to discover and recognize the successor. Thus, particular lines of teaching are formed, in some cases extending over several centuries. Chögyam Trungpa was the eleventh in the teaching lineage known as the Trungpa tülkus.

Once young tülkus are recognized, they enter a period of intensive training in the theory and practice of the Buddhist teachings. Trungpa Rinpoche (*Rinpoche* is an honorific title meaning "precious one"), after being enthroned as supreme abbot of Surmang monastery and governor of Surmang District, began a period of training that would last eighteen years, until his departure from Tibet in 1959. As a Kagyü tülku, his training was based on the systematic practice of meditation and on refined theoretical understanding of Buddhist philosophy. One of the four great lineages of Tibet, the Kagyü is known as the Practice Lineage.

At the age of eight, Trungpa Rinpoche received ordination as a novice monk. After his ordination, he engaged in intensive study and practice of the traditional monastic disciplines as well as in the arts of calligraphy, thangka painting, and monastic dance. His primary teachers were Jamgön Kongtrül of Sechen and Khenpo Kangshar—leading teachers in the Nyingma lineage. In 1958, at the age of eighteen, Trungpa Rinpoche completed his studies, receiving the degrees of *kyorpön* (doctor of divinity) and *khenpo* (master of studies). He also received full monastic ordination.

The late fifties were a time of great upheaval in Tibet. As it became clear that the Chinese Communists intended to take over the country by force, many people, both monastic and lay, fled the country. Trungpa Rinpoche spent many harrowing months trekking over the Himalayas (described in his book *Born in Tibet*). After narrowly escaping capture by the Chinese, he at last reached India in 1959. While in India, Trungpa Rinpoche was appointed to serve as spiritual adviser to the Young Lamas Home School in Dalhousie, India. He served in this capacity from 1959 to 1963.

Trungpa Rinpoche's first opportunity to encounter the West came when he received a Spaulding sponsorship to attend Oxford University. At Oxford he studied comparative religion, philosophy, and fine arts. He also studied Japanese flower arranging, receiving a degree from the Sogetsu School. While in England, Trungpa Rinpoche began to instruct Western students in the dharma (the teachings of the Buddha), and in 1968 he cofounded the Samye Ling Meditation Centre in Dumfriesshire, Scotland. During this period he also published his first two books in English: *Born in Tibet* and *Meditation in Action.*

In 1969, Trungpa Rinpoche traveled to Bhutan, where he entered into a solitary meditation retreat. This retreat marked a pivotal change in his approach to teaching. Immediately upon returning he became a lay person, putting aside his monastic robes and dressing in ordinary Western attire. He also married a young Englishwoman, and together left Scotland and moved to North America. Many of his early students found these changes shocking and upsetting. However, he expressed a conviction that, in order to take root in the West, the dharma needed to be taught free from cultural trappings and religious fascination.

During the seventies America was in a period of political and cultural ferment. It was a time of fascination with the East. Trungpa Rinpoche criticized the materialistic and commercialized approach to spirituality he encountered, describing it as a "spiritual supermarket." In his lectures, and in his books *Cutting Through Spiritual Materialism* and *The Myth of Freedom,* he pointed to the simplicity and directness of the practice of sitting meditation as the way to cut through such distortions of the spiritual journey.

During his seventeen years of teaching in North America, Trungpa Rinpoche developed a reputation as a dynamic and controversial teacher. Fluent in the English language, he was one of the first lamas who could speak to Western students directly, without the aid of a translator. Traveling extensively throughout North America and Europe, Trungpa Rinpoche gave hundreds of talks and seminars. He established major centers in Vermont, Colorado, and Nova Scotia, as well as many smaller meditation and study centers in cities throughout North America and Europe. Vajradhatu was formed in 1973 as the central administrative body of this network.

In 1974, Trungpa Rinpoche founded The Naropa Institute, which became the only accredited Buddhist-inspired university in North America. He lectured extensively at the Institute, and his book *Journey without Goal* is based on a course he taught there. In 1976, he established the Shambhala Training program, a series of weekend programs and seminars that provides instruction in meditation practice within a secular setting. His book *Shambhala: The Sacred Path of the Warrior* gives an overview of the Shambhala teachings.

In 1976, Trungpa Rinpoche appointed Ösel Tendzin (Thomas F. Rich) as his Vajra Regent, or dharma heir. Ösel Tendzin worked closely with Trungpa Rinpoche in the administration of Vajradhatu and Shambhala Training. He taught extensively from 1976 until his death in 1990 and is the author of *Buddha in the Palm of Your Hand.*

Trungpa Rinpoche was also active in the field of translation. Working with Francesca Fremantle, he rendered a new translation of *The Tibetan Book of the Dead,* which was published in 1976. Later he formed the Nalanda Translation Committee, in order to translate texts and liturgies for his own students as well as to make important texts available publicly.

In 1979 Trungpa Rinpoche conducted a ceremony empowering his son Ösel Rangdröl Mukpo as his successor in the Shambhala lineage. In 1995 His Holiness Penor Rinpoche, supreme head of the Nyingma lineage, enthroned him as *Sakyong,* "earth protector." He is now known as Sakyong Mipham Rinpoche.

Trungpa Rinpoche was also known for his interest in the arts and particularly for his insights into the relationship between contemplative discipline and the artistic process. His own art work included calligraphy, painting, flower arranging, poetry, playwriting, and environmental installations. In addition, at The Naropa Institute he created an educational atmosphere that attracted many leading artists and poets. The exploration of the creative process in light of contemplative training continues there as a provocative dialogue. Trungpa Rinpoche also published two books of poetry: *Mudra* and *First Thought Best Thought.*

Trungpa Rinpoche's published books represent only a fraction of the rich legacy of his teachings. During his seventeen years of teaching in North America, he crafted the structures necessary to provide his students with thorough, systematic training in the dharma. From introductory talks and courses to advanced group retreat practices, these programs emphasize a balance of study and practice, of intellect and intuition. Students at all levels can pursue their interest in meditation and the Buddhist path through these many forms of training. Senior students of Trungpa Rinpoche continue to be involved in both teaching and meditation instruction in such programs. In addition to his extensive teachings in the Buddhist tradition, Trungpa Rinpoche also placed great emphasis on the Shambhala teachings, which stress the importance of mind training as distinct from religious practice; community involvement and the creation of an enlightened society; and appreciation of one's day-to-day life.

Trungpa Rinpoche passed away in 1987, at the age of forty-seven. He is survived by his wife, Diana, and five sons. His eldest son, Sakyong Mipham

Rinpoche, succeeds him as president and spiritual head of Vajradhatu, now known as Shambhala International. By the time of his death, Trungpa Rinpoche had become known as a pivotal figure in introducing dharma to the Western world. The joining of his great appreciation for Western culture and his deep understanding of his own tradition led to a revolutionary approach to teaching the dharma, in which the most ancient and profound teachings were presented in a thoroughly contemporary way. Trungpa Rinpoche was known for his fearless proclamation of the dharma: free from hesitation, true to the purity of the tradition, and utterly fresh. May these teachings take root and flourish for the benefit of all sentient beings.

MEDITATION CENTERS AND RESOURCES

For further information regarding meditation or inquiries about a dharma center near you, please contact one of the following centers:

Karmê Chöling
RR 1, Box 3
Barnet, VT 05821
(802) 633–2384

Rocky Mountain Shambhala Center
4921 County Road 68C
Red Feather Lakes, CO 80545
(303) 881–2184

Shambhala Europe
Wilhelmstrasse 20
Marburg, D-35037
Germany
(49#6421) 17020

Shambhala International
1084 Tower Road
Halifax, N.S. B3H 2Y5
Canada
(902) 425–4275

Many talks and seminars are available in cassette tape format. For information, call or write:

Kalapa Recordings
1084 Tower Road
Halifax, N.S. B3H 2Y5
Canada
(902) 421–1550

The Vajradhatu Archives keeps a registry of the ownership of original manuscripts, tapes, and works of art by Chögyam Trungpa so that they can be located for research and exhibit purposes. For further information, or to register an item, call or write:

Vajradhatu Archives
1084 Tower Road
Halifax, N.S. B3H 2Y5
Canada
(902) 421–2696

The Naropa Institute is an accredited, Buddhist-inspired college and graduate school that utilizes the principles of dharma art and of contemplative education in its educational approach. For information about Naropa, write or call:

The Naropa Institute
2130 Arapahoe Ave.
Boulder, CO 80302
(303) 444–0202

For information about a magazine published by students of Chögyam Trungpa, focusing on meditation and the contemplative arts, contact:

Shambhala Sun
P.O. Box 399, Halifax Central
Halifax, N.S. B3J 2P8
Canada
(902) 422–8404

BOOKS BY
CHÖGYAM TRUNGPA

The Art of Calligraphy: Joining Heaven and Earth

Born in Tibet

Crazy Wisdom

Cutting Through Spiritual Materialism

The Dawn of Tantra
by Herbert V. Guenther and Chögyam Trungpa

First Thought Best Thought: 108 Poems

Glimpses of Abhidharma

The Heart of the Buddha

Illusion's Game: The Life and Teaching of Naropa

Journey without Goal: The Tantric Wisdom of the Buddha

The Life of Marpa the Translator
Translated by the Nālandā Translation Committee under the direction of Chögyam
Trungpa

The Lion's Roar: An Introduction to Tantra

Meditation in Action

Mudra

The Myth of Freedom and the Way of Meditation

Orderly Chaos: The Mandala Principle

The Path Is the Goal: A Basic Handbook of Buddhist Meditation

The Rain of Wisdom: The Essence of the Ocean of True Meaning
Translated by the Nālandā Translation Committee under the direction of Chögyam
Trungpa

Shambhala: The Sacred Path of the Warrior

The Tibetan Book of the Dead: The Great Liberation through Hearing in the Bardo
Translated with commentary by Francesca Fremantle and Chögyam Trungpa

Training the Mind and Cultivating Loving-Kindness

138   *Transcending Madness: The Experience of the Six Bardos*

INDEX